A Lucky Monkey on the Hashish Trail

The planet earth is Paradise and we're lucky monkeys to be livin on it.
— Les Vegas — Half a Century Boy

Everyday scene
(collection of the author)

This Book is from the Lucky Monkey series.

Les Braunstein

ISBN: 978-1629670386
Library of Congress Control Number: 2014958473

Table of Contents

The author at twenty-five
(Photo by David Schmidlapp)

Prologue

These are stories from my real life. Why would you want to read them? They're stories of a young kid who was privileged to travel to places that no longer exist. Would you like to travel through Afghanistan when it was magical and fun? How about Ceylon? Plus it was the sixties and the whole world was being turned on its head. Everything was changing (a change that continues today) and the young were taking some level of control over their lives. And there was rock and roll, and then the Beatles. We were fighting the Asian war to a standstill and we floated in space. The world was new. And I, I was a very lucky kid. Just as I finished college I had gotten a song used by Peter Paul and Mary, the biggest folk group in the world. This was a jug band tune called the Blue Frog Song, a song partly about intolerance. Then the Muppets used it. Then Disney, twice. That created a money stream, I called it magic money, that enabled me to buy a 12 string guitar and a Volkswagen bus and begin traveling at will. Wandering the world was my dream. Now I could do it. It was 1967, New York's summer of love. I wandered out to Stony Brook, Long Island where I met and began singing with a rock band, the Soft White Underbelly. For two years we played in the New York underground rock scene, (coming soon *A Lucky Monkey and the Soft White Underbelly*) eventually signing with the Door's label. And then we blew apart. Two years later they were the Blue Oyster Cult and I was on the other side of the Planet. I had traveled across America, taken a freighter to Spain, backpacked around Europe and spent some time with artists in Brussels and Paris, hung out with the gypsies at their annual gathering on the south Coast of France, and lived in the absolutely new society that was Amsterdam in the sixties. (*A Lucky Monkey Wanders America and Europe-1969*) Eventually the Police in Amsterdam told me to get out of the country, and at the same

i

time Patric, a French friend, asked me to drive with him to Istanbul. I couldn't resist. the name was so exotic. I thought it would impress my high school friends to hear I was in Istanbul. So we got into Patric's car, It was a Citroen Duck – the car that looks like a sardine can. Patric's car was painted hot pink, and we headed East in the Pink Duck, passing through Frankfort, Bavaria, Vienna, and Beograd, then across the top of Greece into Istanbul, Turkey.

Istanbul

Yes, Istanbul is the real thing. As a boy I had pictured exotic lands based on illustrations in story books. In China (the East) there would be pagodas, Europe would have cathedrals and castles. In Africa there would be mud huts. And in the Middle East (halfway to the Far East) there would be towers and domes. I had seen no signs of this till now, except for some pretty little white and blue domed Christian churches along the Greek coast. Here in Istanbul they were in full flower.

The Blue Mosque – Istanbul, Turkey
(Bigstock Images)

The Muslims are spectacular architects. Buildings in Istanbul, whether from afar, where they are so dramatic, or up close where they are covered with tiny tiles forming mosaics with musical intensity, are the equal of any great buildings anywhere. Here in Istanbul the mosques were incredible visions. Some, like western churches, were

1

places where people without much money had seen their last coins taken by their religious leaders to build these grand tributes to God, or more exactly to the religion which also meant to the priests who had demanded those coins. But in this vision the people's oppressed and moneyless lives were not a problem, in fact would be redeemed, because they would soon be dead, and all of this would be paid back in *heavenly riches*. Interesting deal. Others were grand palaces built by Sultans, and were opulent and full of jewels, with giant kitchens and quarters for the harem and the eunuchs.

Interior of the Blue Mosque – Istanbul
(Bigstock Images)

Anyway, this city was the first place I had been immersed in all this and it was like a dream. Istanbul had been Constantinople and the center of Christianity at one time, but when the Muslims had taken over, the skyline had changed from steeples to domed mosques and their minarets in every direction. Several times a day, people all around you laid out a prayer mat and knelt toward Mecca and prayed, while the call to prayer was sung simultaneously in every direction from every minaret, amplified electrically, adding an odd new third millennium texture to the moment.

I said my goodbyes to Patric and like all Western travelers I made my way to the Pudding Shop, an institution on the road to the East, a place where you could get both dessert and all the information you needed as to what to see and do and watch out for. I had a coffee and a pastry that was like a deconstructed baclava. Turkish coffee is tasty but comes with sludge on the bottom, so, in my mind, you never get to take that final satisfying sip. I spoke to others and I looked at the many postings on the wall and I quickly had a hotel close by. Also, there was hash available for the first time. Hash and dope were always somewhat available because people you met were carrying, but here in Istanbul people came up to you and offered to sell you a big hunk of local hash and that was new. The first place like it on the Hashish Trail. But there was something else going on here. Although hash was available and cheap, it was also said that travelers were being arrested and thrown into Turkish prisons for possession, and kept there a long time under unhappy conditions. At first it was a little hard to assess the risk. (It was years before people saw the Turkish prison system in Midnight Express.) I definitely wanted to score some of this Turkish hash but ... Eventually I bought some, not from a local (he could turn you in) but from a fellow traveler (he could too.) It was pretty cheap, maybe $20 dollars, and I got a good sized lump of brown hash and took it up to my room.

My room was a small cell with a bed and a window. The bathroom down the hall was a little room with a hole in the floor where you pissed and shat. There wasn't any alternative unless you went to a big international hotel, and even there, I heard, the bathrooms were usually the same.

I went up to my room and heated the hash with a match and crumbled it into a little tobacco and pressed it into the bowl of a carrot pipe. I lay back on my bed and enjoyed the taste and high of this new smoke. Well I enjoyed it for a minute. Then a paranoia began to float in. I knew by now that both things were really true – the hash was good and available, and people were getting busted. At first I figured it was just big dealers getting arrested but every few days we heard that someone we knew from the pudding shop had been busted. I began to see that arresting Westerners was a business out here. Cops would bust anyone they could because it would mean that the kid would have to send home for money to buy his way out. And the Turks had a rep (was it earned? I didn't know.) as a cruel people who would take full advantage of having you locked up. I started thinking about the scene in Lawrence of Arabia where Turks capture Peter O'Toole and do unspeakable things to him. What things? The film wasn't clear about this but they were obviously very cruel. I started to hear the sound of boots on the stairs and without waiting an instant I got up and went into the bathroom and threw the hash down the hole. "Hmmmn," I thought, "I guess that's why they call it shit." ("This is good shit, man".) The police never arrived to take me away but I was relieved it was gone.

I had been expecting some money. I was almost out. I'd been living on a few hundred dollars from Blue Frog royalties I'd brought with me from New York. Traveling for me, back then, was generally running around six to fifteen dollars a day. I usually had a ten dollar or less stay at a hotel, (five dollars if I split it) maybe another four dollars for food. A few dollars for a bus or train. That was it. I was going through my money slowly but when you run out far away from home, you're out, there's no one to turn to and you're no better off than any beggar on the street. The only way I could receive money was to have a family lawyer, Milton Teicher, who was receiving my royalties, wire money to a bank or an American Express office somewhere along the route. Normally checks couldn't be cashed anywhere, and even with money orders they usually wanted to pay in local currency (rarely the best deal) but the American Express office would pay you in American Express travelers checks which you could then cash at the big hotels. I had known I was heading for Istanbul and I had mailed instructions to Milton to take whatever was there (I thought I could have six or seven hundred dollars, maybe more) and send one third to my mother, one third to Kippy (my old girlfriend, I still owed her a couple hundred on her credit card) and the rest to me when I told him where.

I expected that Milton's letter would be waiting for me at the main American Express office in Taxim Square. So I went up there and stood on line with the rest of the travelers and a man shuffled through the letters in a box and found mine. Before I opened it I went outside and bought some street food from a vendor. I had found that you could get something like a Sloppy Joe that was seasoned deliciously and wrapped in a flat bread, so I bought one and sat down on a wall to eat and read my letter. Here's what it said -

August 24, 1970

Mr. Lester (sic) Braunstein
American Express
Istanbul, Turkey

Dear Les:

Last time I heard from Kippy was a day before you finished the first quarter. She told me about your birthday, so congratulations.

Your letter presented minor difficulties in deciphering because of the intrusion of the horse, carriage and violinist on the face of the Austrian Airlines ticket envelope. But your contentment came through and I'm happy for you.

I received the following payments:

April 29, 1970: Pepamar Music, $490.86

July 13, 1970: ASCAP, 277.25

August 17, 1970: Pepemar Music, 2728.85

As you instructed I delivered the first Pepemar check ($490.86) to Kippy. From the last check I will send Mother and Kippy $900 each as you instructed.

Since you apparently will not feel comfortable unless you pay a fee, I will charge you 5% and will retain $175.00.

American Express does not have a paying office in Ankara and since you could not cash my check there I suggest you wire me where or to what foreign bank you want me to wire your money and I will do so immediately.

A total of $3,496.96 has been received. The following are charged against such receipts.

Kippy: $490.86

Kippy: $900.00

Pompie: $900.00

M.Teicher: $175.00

Les: $1,031.00

ASCAP informed me that you were elected to writer membership on April 30th. I have received your membership pin and other printed matter from them. Please let me know if you want this forwarded.

Les, please acknowledge receipt of this letter so I will know you have heard from me. I hope you continue to enjoy your travels and return home with an armful of inspired hits.

Fondly,
Milton

I sat, all by myself on that wall in Taxim Square. I read that line again – Pepamar Music $2,728.85 and I laughed. Magic Money. And I laughed.

MILTON S. TEICHER

ATTORNEY AT LAW

EMPIRE STATE BUILDING
350 FIFTH AVENUE
NEW YORK, N. Y. 10001
(212) 563-2323

August 24, 1970

Mr. Lester Braunstein
American Express
Istanbul, Turkey

Dear Les:

Last time I heard from Kippy was a day before you finished the first quarter. She told me about your birthday, so belated congratulations.

Your letter presented minor difficulties in deciphering because of the intrusion of the horse, carriage and violinist on the face of the Austrian Airlines ticket envelope. But your contentment came through and I'm happy for you.

I received the following payments:

April 29, 1970   Pepamar Music $490.86
July 13, 1970   ASCAP   277.25
August 17, 1970   Pepamar Music   2728.85

As you instructed I delivered the first Pepamar check ($490.86) to Kippy. From the last check I will send mother and Kippy $900.00 each as you instructed.

Since you apparently will not feel comfortable unless you pay a fee, I will charge you 5% and will retain $175.00.

It was here in Istanbul that a traveler gave me a copy of Future Shock, by Alvin Toffler. In it he laid out clearly what I had been feeling, hard evidence that this time was unlike any time before. Here are some passages from Future Shock (1969):

"A growing body of reputable opinion asserts that the present moment represents nothing less than the second great divide in human history, comparable in magnitude only with the first great break in historic continuity, the shift from barbarism to civilization."

and ...

"If the last 50,000 years of man's existence were divided into lifetimes of approximately 62 years each, there have been about 800 such lifetimes. Of these 800, fully 650 were spent in caves.

Only during the last seventy lifetimes has it been possible to communicate effectively from one lifetime to another – as writing made it possible to do. Only during the last six lifetimes did masses of men ever see a printed word. Only during the last four has it been possible to measure time with any precision. Only in the last two has anyone anywhere used an electric motor. And the overwhelming majority of all the material goods we use in daily life today have been developed in the present, the 800th lifetime.

and ...

In 6,000 BC the fastest travel available was the camel caravan, averaging eight miles per hour. Is was not until about 1,600 BC when the chariot was invented that the maximum speed was raised to roughly twenty miles per hour.

It was not until the 1880s that man, with the help of a more advanced steam locomotive, managed to reach a speed of one hundred miles per hour. It took the human race millions of years to attain that record.

It took only 58 years, however, to quadruple the limit, so that by 1938 airborne man was cracking the 400 mile per hour line. It took a mere twenty year flick of time to double the limit again. And by the 1960s rocket planes approached speeds of 4,000 miles per hour, and men in space capsules were circling the Earth at 18,000 miles per hour.

Plotted on a graph the line representing progress in the past generation would leap vertically off the page." – Future Shock – Alvin Tofler

That was it. That image of that line, sleepy so long, now going vertically off the page was a defining moment for me. Everything I was thinking about the world and change, suddenly confirmed by mathematics. And I looked up and even there in Istanbul the world seemed new.

Not so much the Turks themselves. They had changed their dress and the way they ruled themselves early in the century when Attaturk had ordered them into semi-modernity, but that was it. The real difference here was us. What were all these young Westerners doing here?

A rolling stone. A worn out metaphor, but this kind of ability to wander was a primary characteristic of my gen. We got up and wandered the country and the world. Took all those crazy ideas and infected the whole fucking planet. Oooops.

Picture us like a big puff ball. Growing from seeming nothing to something that gets bigger and bigger, that fills the new media and fills our minds ... and then .... bang! it all explodes, throwing us out like seeds, to fly around the world and seed the planet. Istanbul, the pudding shop, the overland trail to India was filled with us. We saw the world and the world saw us.

★★★★★

I was back in the Pudding Shop. I had wired Milton and told him to wire the money to American Express here in Istanbul where they would be happy to give me travelers checks. Everything should be done in a couple of days. Now what? I didn't know. Go home? Istanbul is kind of the end of the line. It's the end of Europe. The city sits at a point where Europe and Asia almost kiss, separated by only the Straits of Bosphorus. Before the two continents drifted apart it was a river that bisected them, but as they pulled apart, the sea rushed in and created a body of sea between them which is as narrow as 3,000 feet (ten football fields.) On one side Turkey is the doorway to Europe, on the other, Turkey is the first step into Asia.

I had been noticing the travelers here in the Pudding Shop. Half the travelers looked like me or anyone. Half the travelers looked altered. First of all they were pale. Somehow they were both tanned and pale. And they ... I don't know, moved slower. A lot of the women wore saris or something wrapped around them. Some of the men too. And they wore sandals, or went barefoot. It was the people coming back from India. The Straits of Bosphorus was one of those spots that travelers had to pass through if they were headed overland out to the East, which usually meant India. A lot of young people were headed to India, partly for all the usual travel reasons (fun,sun) and then many more because it held out the possibilities of spiritual growth. Many young Westerners had put down their studies or careers in a search for spiritual peace. Whatever the eventual relationship between the Beatles and the Maharishi Mahesh Yogi it was obvious that people were getting something out of being there. Many went to see established gurus (a new word to us then) at ashrams (another one) but just being in India did seem to be life changing for many. And now here they were in the Pudding Shop. Istanbul was the doorway to the East and most travelers there were either going to the East or coming back ... so suddenly, with my pockets about to be overfilled with magic money, I thought ... why not?

Turkish Train

So I was on a train, going east across Turkey. Once we had crossed over onto the continent of Asia the views became long, the distances great. Crossing Turkey was going to take longer than I had thought. About a week, it turned out. Ferries, trains, busses, trains. More busses. three dollar hotels.

If charming Istanbul felt dangerous and sometimes inhospitable, there was to be no let- up until we crossed the rest of Turkey and Iran. Both of these countries were cold to western travelers. It was like taking a deep breath, diving in, knowing there would be no coming up until the Afghan border where things were reputed to be better. Long stretches began now where we were truly distant from our homes, out of contact, in an unfriendly environment, protected only by the hope that lawlessness would be held at bay because it would create too much trouble for the locals if travelers were killed or seriously injured. Although Westerners could be fleeced, that's what you were there for. And you could always be thrown in jail for a drug offense, real or not, where you could buy your way out, if you were lucky.

There was an American guy named Jeff traveling the same direction. He was about 21. Nice guy. Blonde. From an Mi state. He and I were sharing a compartment with a young Brit couple, Penny and Giles. Compartment mates are critical in a long trip. Giles was not so nice. He was generally surly except when he was berating Penny. Making fun of her, that seemed to wake him up. Giles was headed to Iran for a conference where he was going to be quite important. Penny was just "along."

Penny was very sweet. Kind of shy and giggly and didn't seem to take offense. Tall and pretty with short dark hair. Blue eyes.

Outside our windows, Turkey rolls by. Low mountains in the distance change to near mountains shooting straight up at the sky, changing to flat desert. A river appears out the window to the north. It runs along the tracks for a long time. For hours, then almost the whole day, it wanders close and far, zooming and zigzagging across the desert floor. "What's the name of that river?" I ask a conductor. "Meander."

We're cleaning up after lunch when a conductor comes by.

"What should we do with this?" I ask, holding up our bag of trash. The conductor takes the bag. Then he opens the window and throws the bag out onto the desert.

"Hey! Don't do that," I can't help saying. The conductor looks at me as if I'm an idiot, shrugs and leaves.

"Why do you care what he does?" says Jeff. "It's his country."

"It's my world."

"Your world" says Jeff. "Ha ha. That's good. Your world. .....Yeah."

Early that evening we pass a mountain that reminds me of pictures of Mount Ararat in a picture book Bible. It has a very steep profile, and a perfect spot on top to rest an Arc. It looks like the top half of a mountain poking up through a flat sea of silt. It looked to me like there actually had been a flood here. A big one. (To conductor) "What's the name of that mountain?" "Ararat." Oooo, I thought. Turkey. A lot happened here.

★★★★★

Here's what it looked like, maybe this is true (I'm not a geologist though I play one in this paragraph.): Noah's ark latched onto Ararat when it was an island poking up out of a flood, out of a new freshwater ocean. When the rush of water ended, and the levels receded, the mud of the desert became a high plain. Small mountains were covered completely. Towns too. Whether it had been ordained by a vengeful god or just geologic events, the world became something new and flat, halfway up Mount Ararat. It did look like that had happened here.

Later that night we are trying to sleep. The berths are too narrow to sleep on so we all sleep on the compartment floor. It's pretty crowded.

Jeff and Giles sleep against opposite sides of the car with Penny and me in between. I lay on my back being rocked by the train, clukutta-clukutta. I can see moonlight on the beveled edge of the window as I doze toward sleep.........and.....uh what? What's thiiiiiis? A hand in my sleeping bag? Penny. On my leg. Ohhhhhhhhhh beautiful world. Moonlight, clukutta-clukutta, and a stranger girl's hand in my underpants. Reaching for...but not quite reaching...

I yawn and stretch and move a little closer. Her hand circles my saluting cock and just holds it. I don't move. She doesn't move. I glance at her. She appears to be asleep. She isn't. Without seeming to move, I reach out carefully under her blanket, and work my hand up under her t-shirt to her pretty little breast. I find her nipple and just hold it. Squeezing a little. Quietly. She does the same.

And that's the way we ride into the night. I could have popped right away but why? That moment would come. And this moment is deeeelicious. Mmmmm clukutta- clukutta. Clukutta-clukutta.A little while later she slides her hand all the way down and the moment comes.. Oh man, does it come. And I have to be silent. But I guess I am kidding myself about that, because Giles is suddenly snarling at Penny, "Get up. Get over here!" He hisses and drags her over to his other side. He doesn't look at me. This might have happened before. He has nothing to say. He'd run out of bon mo's.

Well, I figured, Giles was lucky to be along.

Letter to Henry – (my brother in law.)

Henry -

After eating some beef the other day in Turkey, (as you may remember from your time here, they eat lots of kebabs and meatball type things) I was feeling, after digesting, sluggish and gross – a little stupid- in fact, rather cow-like. Which set me thinking do we have cow vision while their meat is in our body?

There is a theory which I loosely remember but largely believe – that memory is stored, at least partially, in either the DNA or RNA (I forget which.) The theory runs that when you have an experience it sends a shockwave through the DNA which leaves a trace, a foot-print, peculiar to that experience. When you have a similar experience the traces line up, fully or in part, and you remember. So some part of memory exists within the individual cells.

There was an experiment that I came across when I was working with planaria in high school. Planaria are platyhelminthes, little flat-worms that look like they've got cartoon eyes which make them look cute. There is a classic conditioning exercise done with planaria where the planaria are put in a water chamber and subjected to first a bright light and then an electrical charge. When the charge goes through them they scrunch up. After a while when you turn on the light they scrunch up expecting the charge which means they're trained. All of this is basic conditioning but in one experiment this guy trained the worms then ground them up and fed them to other worms. Far out huh? Then he puts the new worms in the chamber and sure enough they scrunch at the light. So why should it be sur-prising that I feel like a cow after eating beef?

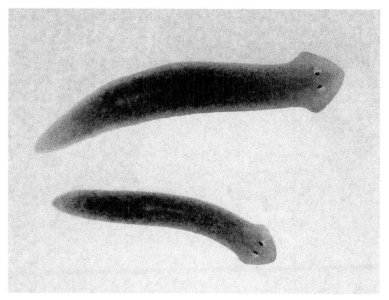

Persia, now calling itself Iran, felt worse than Turkey. This is the place where they supposedly shot people caught with hash, although according to traveler knowledge they only shot their own people, and only when they got caught with large quantities. In any case, there were lots of horror stories, and there was a lot they could do to you short of shooting you anyway.

I didn't spend much time in Iran. The Iranian Tourist Brochure had a pithy line – "It is the immediate aim of the Iranian Tourist Bureau to convince travelers to spend more than 6 days in Iran," which was the time it took to cross overland from Turkey to Afghanistan. I did it in 5. I knew I was missing a lot. But there was a certain air of hostility. They were smiling, but there was a feeling that you didn't want to let these people get anything on you. You don't want to fall into their clutches. And if you were a woman...

One incident along the way was illustrative of what I was seeing. I had gone to the train station in Tehran to buy tickets on a train headed east. Having made my arrangements I was leaving the large ornate Western style station when I noticed a puppy running across the wide station floor searching for a way out. Puppies are the same everywhere. They're babies and as babies have certain physical characteristics that make them adorable to most humans. Is it the way their eyes are close together? Is it the way they stop and regard you with no malice. In any case, though he was a long way across the station from me I saw a puppy that looked in its way like every other puppy I'd ever seen. And it looked like it needed assistance as it tried to flop it's way up the big steps toward the exit and I started to make my way across to help. But no need, since a station guard was there and about to pick it up and put it outside. But no. The guard pulled back his leg and with a vicious swing smashed his leather boot into the little dog and kicked it, not out of the station, but deeper into it, where, without a doubt it had more savage kicks in its near future.

Now I can accept that these people had no respect for dogs and considered them unclean, so don't keep them around or roll around on the carpet with them, but this man had no sense at all that this animal had feelings or maybe that this animal's feelings should be considered at all. He could have used a hit of that Golden Rule. But it was nowhere around.

Anyway, it was with great relief when we drew up to, and were deposited at, the Afghan border. At last. The Famous Fabled East.

Afghanistan

Crossing the border into Afghanistan would seem like a simple enough procedure and was, in fact, simple, and yet it managed to take several hours. How they do this is one of the enduring if not endearing mysteries of the East and something you better get used to. There was a chi shop (tea house) on the Afghani side and once you hassled your way out of Iran you could sit around in there while the Afghanis got it together in their immigration shack and a bus arrived to run you into Herat, about two hours away. Evening was falling. Jeff was checking on the passports and I sat down in the chi shop. I was pretty happy to be there, and happier to be out of Iran, and my joy was made complete when an Afghan kid, about twelve years old, brought me some tea and....

"Hashish?"

The kid is holding up for my perusal something that looks like a hockey puck, maybe three quarters of an inch thick, and about three inches across. I had never seen such a big and, as a matter of fact, beautiful piece of hash. It was dark, almost black, and embossed with some kind of emblem.

"How much?"

"Forty Afghani."

I do the math. I figure I have it wrong. My calculations are telling me this is about fifty cents. I do the math again. Fifty cents. Now, I know I am fresh and naïve out here, but really, how far wrong can I go? I decide to take a flier.

I look around the chi shop. People are sitting around in small groups drinking glasses of Afghan tea and talking. No one is paying any attention to me, but I don't want to roll some up and smoke it right here. This country might be cool about dope but that seems like pushing it. Instead I break off a couple of pieces about the size of a

15

dime (and three quarters of an inch thick) and wash them down with the tea. Then I figure that if it's this easy to get hash, there is no sense carrying it around (I'm not quite over that Turkish/Iranian paranoia) so I decide to give the rest away. Yeah. This will surprise my fellow travelers. I start giving it away and then, when it's almost gone, just to be sure, I eat another piece. If it's amazing for me to buy hash so cheap here in Afghanistan, imagine, I think, how it has to flash these total strangers in the chi shop when I give them hash for free. Free hash at the Afghani border. But the real flash is yet to come.

It is dark as we board the bus, and the effects of what I have eaten have yet to arrive. Jeff and I are sitting in the back of the bus which is filled to capacity with about four fifths Western freaks and one fifth Afghanis and other Easterners. I have changed some money and Jeff hasn't, so I am going to pay for both of us. It's a little over a dollar each. My first inkling that something is up (me) is when, after about half an hour, an Afghan man comes around to collect the bread.

"Two hundred Afghani." he says.

We will ignore the IMPLICATIONS that are immediately apparent to me concerning this Eastern VISITATION and say only that the ENORMOUS task of conjuring up my wallet is suitably capped by the fact that when it appears it contains NO AFGHAN MONEY! Now, this is a situation that would be intriguing to the normally functioning mind. Here is my wallet, which is still on my person, which is filled with great stuff to steal, travelers checks, American dollars, a passport, none of which is disturbed and there is no sign of about six dollars worth of Afghan currency I had stuck in there. I am fascinated.

The Afghan guy somewhat less so. "Hey. Two hundred Afghani!"

There is little time for rumination because the Afghan is demanding his money and Jeffery is getting upset for the both of us. "Ripped off?" ...he sneers at all the villains lurking around us. What are we to do?

But my brain is, needless to say, in overdrive. Time is running out. Options are limited. I take my only shot.

"Will someone lend us two hundred Afs till I can change money tomorrow?"

At first everyone is stunned at my audacity. Lend money (a little over two dollars) to some stranger on a bus in Afghanistan? (I had just given free hash to some of these people.) And then suddenly...

"Here. I'll take care of that."

Someone is giving the man two hundred Afs and I am saying, "Thanks. Follow me around till I can change money tomorrow." And the guy is nodding and smiling, "Yes."

And it is because he is, at that moment, on our side, that I put aside the thought that this guy looks particularly pasty and puffy under the orangish inside bus light and is, in fact, a LARGE WHITE SLUG.

The immediate commotion over and the light put out, I sit back and begin to fully experience the state I am in. I am incapacitated. I am on the far side of wrecked, have left wrecked far far behind. Hmmmmm.

The rest of the people on the bus begin to sing. And such a subtle song. To the non-attuned ear it would seem like they were just talking. But since it is impossible for them to all talk at once, and since there are several language groups represented, they seem to take turns dominating the sound waves, as the bus whirrs and whizzes across the Afghan desert. For instance, you could be listening to the indistinct lazy guffawing of the English and Americans, and when they trail off after some joke, you might hear the first tentative blurp of French as it steps in to see if it has the field. And if the English is truly through, the French will suddenly babble up to immediate sing-songy peaks, with twittering bursts suddenly cut short by an excited swell of Italian. All flaring and mixing and swelling and fading and completely indistinct and at the same time completely understandable and most strange I SEEM TO BE IN CHARGE. It seems to me that I am conducting the ebb and flow, and my fellow travelers seem aware of that and alternately get off on it or are disappointed in it, and after all, I do know for a fact that telepathy exists, and I am in overdrive, so why not? And it is just then that the bus stops, absolutely in the middle of nowhere, in the middle of the desert, in the middle of the night, and they let off an Afghani man, who noticed only by me, begins to run along behind the bus, and I realize that if I don't stop myself I might just make this guy run up to the back window and shoot me through the back of my head and ohhhhhhhhhhhhh!

A great while later, I notice that the music of the bus engine and gears has changed and we must be getting somewhere. Sure enough, we are in Herat. The bus rolls on for a while and eventually turns into a courtyard and stops. As the engine ceases I suddenly realize that something has not ceased with it. That there is a finger running rhythmically around the rim of my hand. I look at the finger touching my hand ....fingering my hand, and then up the arm to see... SLUGMAN! Uuuuugh. Uuuuuugh. Behind rimless glasses Slugman's lashes flicker. He smiles. Uuuuuuuuuugh!

Anyway, I beat it out of the bus only to find that my pack doesn't seem to be among the packs taken down from the roof where I definitely saw it go.

"Isn't that your pack?" says Jeff pointing to an alien looking shape.

"No."

"They stole your pack too?" Jeff is enraged, a true friend. "Those bastards!"

After all the packs are unloaded there is none unclaimed but that one.

"You sure that isn't your pack?"

I re-examine. It does reveal itself to be my pack. Unidentifiable because it was upside down.

A smiling Afghan says, "This way for sleeping."

Everyone is milling around the dark yard, undecided. I follow the smiler. Many follow me. We are led into a dank dark cell. Having led my minions in I immediately walk out – not for me. Eventually I follow some others up onto the roof and I lay down and churn off to sleep.

But no respite for me or you either friend reader. The sun is immediately up and I am being awakened by Slugman.

"Hey!"

"Yuh??"

"Its six o'clock, says Slugman.

"Six?"

"Its six am and I have a bus at eight. Come on. We have to change money."

"At six AM? Nothing will be open."

"We'll see. Come on."

I am, by the way, no less stoned at this point, but to suit Slugman, who after all did lend me the money, I get up and grab my things and stumble down the side of the building and for the next hour Slugman leads me all over town futilely trying to change an American twenty dollar bill and finally leaves me, spitting, "Well, I guess you've got yourself a couple hundred Afs!" (About two dollars and twenty cents.)

And the poor boy (me) spends the next two hours sitting like a wino on the curb, on the far side of Herat, on the far side of the world, with my face in my hands, until I can get it together to find my way back to the hotel roof where I fall out for another half a day, and that's a trip.

Herat and Kandahar

Herat was a city of horses. They trotted up the street in a dance, pulling little carriages. Each carriage was painted all over with pictures and other painted decoration. Every inch. And each truck and bus on the street was illustrated with flowers and animals and little landscaped scenes. Not just a large mural on each side, but every inch of space was covered with these little paintings. It was everywhere, and I'd never seen anything like it. It had a lot to do with my first impression of the country and it's people. I figured that no people with this much art in their lives could be bereft of soul.

And the horses. They were everywhere in this little city and they seemed to be celebrated rather than being viewed as dumb work animals. The people clearly loved their horses in Herat, and between the horses and the painted vehicles, the street scene was surprisingly gay.

That is, except for the women. Whereas women in the previous Moslem countries had their faces covered with scarves, these Afghan women wear the burka, a one piece cloth shroud, usually black, that covers them head to toe, with only a small woven grill allowing them to see out. When they appear on the streets at all, they hurry from corner to corner like black shadows. Shades. But mostly, not on the streets at all. Though I thought I liked these people, it was easy to see that the women, were under complete domination.

Afghani women in the Burkha

As a traveler I took it for granted that each new culture would show me something I had never imagined. Would have aspects that were unknown to me and hard to understand through Western eyes, but after a couple months in Afghanistan I knew that this was, in fact, a terrible burden and a lasting problem, not only for the women, but for their society in total. I had no contact with women in Afghanistan. I did not talk to one in a market or a chi shop. They weren't there. All my conversations were with men and boys. Women were owned and hidden away. Respected and revered possibly, if one were to accept the literature, but totally without control over their existences beyond the home. And the homes were walled compounds.

I awoke the afternoon of my first day in Herat, back on the roof, having finally shaken off the effects of my border experience. How I had found my way back to the little hotel, I don't know. I could see from there that Herat was an oasis town with some greenery. That had been scarce along the recent journey. The sun was high in the sky. My bones were warming. From the street I heard the clop and jingle of the horses mixed in with the usual traffic sounds. And everywhere was an aroma that I was to come to associate with Afghanistan, the smell of small fires, burning everywhere along the roadsides, where men cooked little kabobs over small braziers. This smell was so ever-present that years later, a smell like that would summon up an immediate olfactory memory, and I would be back there in that so different place.

Because this place was different, in all the ways a traveler dreams. Exotic dress, architecture, landscape, attitude, sounds, food, and here even smell. And home so far away. That is a feeling that is harder to find today. In most places now, though you be on the far side of the planet, you carry inside the feeling that home, in an emergency, is a plane and a day away. That wasn't true for travelers at that time. We had come overland and would return that way, and our homes were months away. Telephoning was not possible. Even in Italy phoning America had required long periods at a special telephone station. Here in the East there was nothing like that. Contact with home meant a letter waiting for you at a pre-ordained American Express office in a bigger city than this. Email? Not yet a madman's dream.

I got up and descended into the hotel, drawn by the sounds of laughing and ….the smell of burnt toast? I peeked into an open room. A couple guys were sitting around. They were English and I was going to get to know them very well. Barry and Dave. Barry was reclining on his bed. He looked like Rod Stewart (though I hadn't yet ever seen Rod Stewart). What was fine about Barry was that he was always laughing. He had come all the way out to Afghanistan to enjoy an indulgent moment in the sun and he was having that. Dave was a man's man. Maybe a hod carrier, one of those British laborer guys. He didn't claim to be the brains of the team but he had a great heart. They were having tea and burning a piece of nan, the local bread, over a small brass contraption that looked like something a Brit archeologist would take on expedition.

I am stumbling in from (you will remember) a 24 hour hashish stunning and a sleep on a roof.

"Hi," (I croak) "Do you think I could have a cup of tea?"

They look up at me ..... and laugh and laugh. Dave goes and gets me a cup.

"Want some honey? No proper milk, just this stuff." He holds up a container of powdered milk.

"Everything, thanks."

"You look like you could use some of this," says Barry who is holding up a very fat joint.

"No thanks. I ate some at the border and I've just come down."

This sends them into more laughter. They know about eating this hash.

"Really," laughs Barry, "this will make you feel better."

Then for the first time of many many times in Afghanistan, I have a smoke against my better judgement. Hmmnnnnn. But all we do is laugh and tell traveler's tales for the next few hours and everything is good.

The next day we all took the bus to Kandahar, halfway across Afghanistan. Once again some mountains we passed looked like they were half buried in a sea of silt.

We had just gotten to a hotel and secured a large room together (about four dollars) when Dave suddenly jumped up and ran to 'the loo'. (Brit talk for the bathroom.) Let's describe the loo. Another hole in the floor. That was pretty much it, except for a little water faucet on the wall for washing up. OK. Dave seemed to have contracted the "shits." That was funny for a few minutes until one by one we were all smacked down and brought low, each of us by the same malady. Sorry to say, my friends, but this was the beginning of a state of being that would not end until we left that entire part of the world. That's why those travelers coming back from India looked so white. Yes, my friends, I had the shits from that day forward, for about a year, until I arrived back in the West. You had diareaha for a year? I hear you asking. Yes. And we're not going to discuss it much, except to say that it becomes a fact of life that you live with and try not to mind. Not that day though in Kandahar. The outset of this problem is the most intense, and for the next two days, we would return from the toilet, sit down on our beds, then the moment we stretched out our bodies to lie down, the train would start down the tracks and we were back in the little room. Nausea too, those first days.

After a few days things had finally slowed down to where we thought we could take a bus on the next, and we headed for Kabul, our real destination.

Kabul

I stand in front of the Khyber Restaurant which is located on a traffic circle. Traffic today is donkeys, painted trucks and busses, all different kinds of motorized and bicycle rickshaws and now, an amazingly large water buffalo. Two men walk it around the circle, one pulls on a rope in a ring through it's nose, and the other flips its tail up and prods it with a stick up it's ass. Apparently the only prodding the thing can notice.

I enter the Khyber Restaurant. It is big and light, more Western than most other buildings in Kabul. I sit down at a table and a man brings me a menu.

"Thanks. Tashakoor." I examine the menu.

"Hamburger. And french fries."

"French rice?" asks the Afghan waiter

"Fries." I say, "French fried potatoes."

"Potatoes?"

"Yes. Potatoes."

"And rice?"

"No. No rice. Only potatoes. French fried potatoes." I show the man on the menu.

"OK. OK." He's getting annoyed.

"And one hamburger."

"Ham-mer-gur." he attempts.

"Yeah. And ketchup. Ketchup?"

The man walks away without replying. A woman enters the restaurant. Western women rarely wore the burka and weren't expected to. After all they were already whores by virtue of their lives and their Western ways, infidels and unclean. But it was rare that they flaunted their normal way of dress. No mini-skirts on these streets. Often they wore lovely large cloth wraps, some were like saris, some were just large shawls, and they wrapped them around their bodies so they were fully covered, although their faces were still in everyone's faces. This one is wearing many layers of colored cloth. Not dark but brightly colored like the Koochi tribeswomen on the desert. Completely covered but very eye-catching. She is lovely but a little distracted looking. She looks across the restaurant for something. Her eyes stop when they meet mine. She comes across the room to me.

"Mind if I join you?" (She's British.)

"Not at all. Cup of tea?" (I'm Cary Grant.)

"Have you seen the tea?" (Oh good. Katherine Hepburn.)

"Served in a glass with a pile of sugar in the bottom." I actually liked it but the Brits wouldn't touch it.

"Just like Mother's. I'll have some coffee."

"Its powdered coffee."

"That's all right."

"Powdered milk."

"We're in Kabul. Does it have any lamb fat? "

"That's extra." I say. She sits.

"I suppose it seems a bit forward of me to come over," she says.

"I don't think so. There's a gravitational pull between travelers in far flung regions."

"Yes. There is. And forces that spin them apart."

"Centripetal," I say.

"Inertial," she says and we both laugh.

"I'm Sheila. Are you a poet or musician? Some kind of artist?"

"I'm a singer. Musicians don't usually consider singers musicians. And I write poetry but I'm not sure that automatically makes you a poet.

"Singer with a band?"

"The Soft White Underbelly, in New York."

"I don't think I know..."

"We nova'd before we went super. How about you?"

"I got to go super for a while, but then ... boom."

"What did you do?"

"I had a boutique in London. Granny Takes a Trip."

"Hey. I read about that place in Life Magazine." I had, and I have to be impressed by this.

"Yeah. That's the one."

"You did outfits for the Stones. "

"Yeah," says Sheila, "Brian Jones. Then Mick. And the Who and the Beatles.

"Wow."

"Pink Floyd."

"Those must have been good times."

(From the Vintage Fashion Guild website, re – Granny Takes a Trip

At the end of 1965, the previous owners of a little vintage clothing stall opened a shop called Granny Takes a Trip in King's Road, London. It was run by Victorian clothing collector Sheila Cohen, her boyfriend, the painter Nigel Waymouth and his friend John Pierse. It began as a place for hippies to get hold of antique clothing, but evolved into creating it's own unique designs and styles influenced by fashion of the past.

When the unique designs became a major element of Pink Floyd's shows, their clientele soon expanded to include the Small Faces, the Byrds, Jimi Hendrix, the Who, the Rolling Stones and the Beatles.

Originally decked out as a psychedelic New Orleans bordello with an old horn gramophone, the facade of the shop became just as famous as the clothes. Beginning with giant and fierce blow-ups of Native American Indian chiefs Low Dog and Kicking Bear designed by Nigel and Michael English, quickly followed by the famous pop art portrait of Jean Harlow, and finally the front end of a 1947 Dodge was painted yellow and bolted to the front window.

The flat above the shop was occupied by a student who later gained fame as the notorious writer Salman Rushdie. He remembered the place as " pitch dark. The air was heavy with incense and patchouli oil and also the aromas of what the police call "certain substances .... It was a scary place." When John and Yoko arrived outside the shop in their Rolls Royce one evening he ventured downstairs to introduce himself. When Sheila Cohen answered the door to him she said "Don't you know the art of conversation's dead man?" and slammed the door in his face.

Sheila Cohen at
Granny Takes a Trip
(London)

"Yes. Very good times. (She trails off) Then Boom!"

"Nova."

"Supernova. And then I flew out here. But I don't want to talk about that. And here's your food."

The waiter brings over the food on a tray. He places the plates in front of me.

"I'll have a coffee," says Sheila to the waiter.

The waiter doesn't look at her. He barely grunts in reply and goes off.

"What is that?" says Sheila looking at my plate. "A hamburger?"

"This, My Dear, is the only hamburger I have seen east of the Bosphorus."

"That must make your Yank heart flutter."

"Oh yes, but the illusion won't last long."

"Illusion?"

"That this is a hamburger."

"It looks like a hamburger."

"That's it's trick. It looks like a burger but it's not made of cow."

"No?"

"My guess is water buffalo. You see its greyish hue."

"Ugh."

"And rubbery texture."

"I'll take your word for it."

"And when you eat it, it makes you burp burps that taste like farts."

"And you do this repeatedly?"

I do actually. "I usually give myself four or five days to forget. Then I'm back."

"It's that American spirit."

"Yes. And the ketchup is obviously made from beets not tomatoes, but they figure its red, so that should be good enough and the Western fools will eat it. And we are so starved for some good old American food, or something even *like* American food, that we do."

The kid's working hard. Usually he gets by on being a rock singer, playing his guitar, but this girl's been up in the big time. She's being nice but she's been hanging with Lennon and McCartney. So he starts peddling fast.

"But I think all of our stomachs would be working better if we acclimated our selves properly."

"Acclimated."

"Yeah, we travel too fast." I'm warming to the story. I'm in my faux scientist mode. "We don't give our bodies a chance to get used to the bacteria and such that we are encountering. Busses and trains rush us hundreds of miles. Planes are worse. Take you for instance. One day you were in London and the next Kabul. That's got to be a shock to your system."

"And what's your solution?"

"I would say that the best way to travel would be on foot. I guess a horse would be OK. Yeah, I've been thinking I'll look for a horse and maybe try traveling that way for a while."

"Hey," says Sheila, "my friends here are traders and they all have horses. They can help you get a horse."

"Oh yeah?"

"Yeah, come on back to the house with me and I'm sure they can set you up."

"Uhh. Great."

★ ★ ★ ★ ★

I'm in a trader's villa in Kabul. Sheila and I are sitting with David and Helen, husband and wife English traders. We are sitting on cushions and eating a sumptuous feast being served by an Afghan man and boy. We are surrounded by outlandishly beautiful Afghani goods and crafts.

"This place is amazing," I say with true admiration. "How did you find all these things?"

"We've spent a lot of time here. This is our eighth trip out," says David.

"Ninth, I think," says Helen.

"Ninth. And we've traveled a lot around the country. There's no place like Afghanistan for beautiful crafts and arts."

"Wood carvings," continues Helen, "Weavings. Jewelry. Daggers. All so very lovely."

I've noticed the same thing. "'Occasionally I've seen a tool," I say, "a ladle maybe or a pot, and a crack has been repaired with a little piece of brass taken from somewhere and worked in, in a way that's more beautiful than ever."

"Yes," says David, "they believe anything worth doing is worth doing with art."

"And," says Helen, "everything we have here is the finest Afghan quality. First quality, the Afghans say."

"Of course, that's not the principle export of Afghanistan," I say.

"You mean hash? That's another story," says David. "Trading in hashish requires more thought then most Westerners put into it. They think that they just come out here and buy some nice hash, wrap it very well, maybe hide it in a lamp, and ship it home."

"And that doesn't work?"

"Rarely. First of all you have to give yourself the time to know your sources".

"Make a few trips out here," I say.

"Yes," says David. "Otherwise, they might sell you the hash then sell you out."

"And most important," Helen adds, "Baksheesh."

"Bribes?"

"Baksheesh is so much more than that." David pours more tea. "It's an understanding of how the economy works out here. Everything has a price, usually very cheap by our standards, but above that is the..”

“Grease for the wheels?”

“Yes, and baksheesh is also a sign of respect. That you understand this is the man with the knowledge and power to help you. You pay him this respect and he helps you accomplish your task. If he’s the proper person he will share his baksheesh with all the others down the line.”

“And your hash gets through.”

“Not us, of course,” says David. “We are just traders in fine goods and crafts.”

Sheila excuses herself and gets up and leaves the room.

Helen leans toward me. “We’re so happy that Sheila has found you. Do you know much of her story?”

“I just know that she had a successful boutique in London, but now its gone.”

David and Helen look at each other.

“Yes,” says Helen. “It’s gone and the experience has....”

“Unmoored her,” says David.

“Yes, says Helen. “She’s a bit adrift now and she’s out here for a ... rest cure.”

“She just needs a little time,” says David.

“And friends,” says Helen. “Will you be her friend?”

I have to think for a moment. It seems more important than it had a moment before. “‘Yes.. I think so.”

“Good,” says David as Sheila returns with something in her hand. “Ah. The chillum. Have you ever smoked a chillum, Les?”

“No. Is it some kind of pipe?”

“More than a pipe. It is a religious article of the Indian Sadhu.

“Sadhu?” I hadn’t heard of the Sadhu.

“Holy men,” says Sheila.

“Sometimes revered crazy men,” says Helen.

Indian Sadhu – smoking a chillum
(Bigstock Images)

"You heat the hash a little...(David sticks a chunk of hash on the point of an Afghan knife and heats it over a flame) and then you crumble it generously into some tobacco.(he does this) put a little stone inside and fill the chillum. Then you cup your hands around the bottom, and you pull the smoke in between your palms. It takes a little practice."

David wraps his hands around the chillum and Sheila leans over with a match. "Boom Shankar!!" he calls out. Sheila lights it as he draws.

"Boom Shankar." the women respond.

"What's that?" I ask.

"That's what the Sadhus say when they take a hit," Helen says taking the chillum.

"What does it mean?"

"Its a thank you," says David, "to the gods, for the sacrament of hashish.

Helen adds, "And an invitation to others to share in the gift."

She refills the chillum and passes it to me. I try to wrap my hands around it. With a little effort I feel satisfied and Helen lights it for me.

"Boom Shankar!" I pull through my fingers and the chillum glows.

Every one says, "Boom Shankar!

I hold the big hit and slowly exhale.

"Boom Sha-boom," my mouth says. We laugh.

David is talking, "So, Sheila says you're looking for a horse."

"Well..." Slow down pardner, I'm thinking.

Sheila says, "Les feels that he will stay healthier if he travels by horse. More *acclimated*."

Now Helen chimes in, "That sounds right. Well, we should be able to fix you up."

"Fix me up?"

"With a horse," says Helen brightly. "They have such fine horses here in Afghanistan. They breed them for the Bushkazi."

"Bushkazi?" everything seems to be moving a little fast.

"Its like polo," says David, "only instead of a ball they use a dead goat."

"Its very rough," says Helen. She's getting excited. "And the horses are magnificent. Tough and strong and fearless. We'll get the trader out tomorrow." Trader? Tomorrow? "He'll get you a good one."

"I'd need a small horse," I'm kind of whining. "That would be best for me. "

"We'll tell the trader," says David.

Sheila gets up.

"I think its time to turn in."

She reaches out to me. I get up and take her hand. She walks me out and down the corridor into a room with a big fluffy bed covered with red, orange and purple Afghan pillows. The room is lit by candles and oil lamps. Sheila sits on the bed and holds her hand out to me. I sit by her and look into her eyes. My mouth is drawn toward hers, she is lovely. And sweet and smart and vulnerable. And her desire for me makes her even more attractive.

"Sheila are you sure you're up for..."

Sheila unlaces the top of her dress exposing her full round breasts. She pulls my face into them. I can't resist, even for a moment. They are lightly perfumed with Eastern oils and light perspiration. My face slides down in between them then across them and my tongue licks her nipple and she hums. I fall onto her and try to keep myself slow as I run my hand up her leg. She is very soft and womanly and I am gone again.

★ ★ ★ ★ ★

Here's why I wanted a small horse – I was never much of an athlete. I guessed it was that coordination thing that I didn't have. At summer camp in the fifties, when I was about seven, I had a little more than my share of being picked last. So one day I went over to the camp stables to see about horseback riding. Maybe I wouldn't need too many athletic skills for that, although it did seem kind of dangerous. Next thing I knew they had put me on top of this giant ... animal ... where, if the thing noticed me at all, I was probably just like a bug or a little spider monkey on his back. The stable boys handed me the reins. Were they kidding? Who was going to hold on to the horse?!! This one stableboy, thinking he was helping said...

"Don't worry. A horse has this lens in his eye that make you look giant to him. He's probably scared of you."

Oh. That's great, I was thinking. Just another wild card to throw into this potentially fatal situation.

After a few weeks I had gotten somewhat used to mounting these things. I had learned to walk them around the corral and endure a trot for a second or two. The trot made you bounce up and down in the saddle which smacked you in the ass. They'd make you hold that for a short while and then let you relax into the walk again. On one or two occasions they'd made all the horses run, gallop, but that was very scary.

I did like hanging out at the stables, though. They made you shovel out the stalls as part of learning horsemanship but I didn't mind that. I liked the smell of horse shit. A little cowshit too, in a whiff on a summer night. And it was relatively quiet at the stables compared to the basket ball court where you would whirl around in a bunch of guys screaming for you to throw the ball which you would immediately lose and just as likely get smacked in the face with.

Toward the end of the season at camp was always Color War. (They had to dump that name in the sixties when it would suggest something else.) Everyone in the camp was divided up into the blue team or the gold team and one half of the camp played the other in everything from baseball and archery, to singing and putting on skits. The skits were pretty good and the counselors wrote songs that were good too. Like ..

"There was a counselor of Musketeers (the other guys)
Who worked at camp for so many years
The only thing he did for fun
Was drive the guests to Binghamton
And as he drove them out along two-twelve
Into their finances he would delve
And he'd find out in just one trip
How much they'd give him for a tip" (anonymous)

There was a big all-camp assembly on the main lawn one afternoon in the middle of this. I had been told to report to the horse guys who were off to the side behind the dining hall with one of the little Shetland Ponies.

"Hey Les. Com'ere. Here's what we're gonna do." They were putting an oversized blue coat on me as they spoke. "These three big guys in Musketeer costumes are gonna go riding across the field on big horses and then this little guy is gonna gallup after them on a little pony and chase them away. Funny."

"Uhhh."

"Get on the pony." They hoisted me, objecting, onto the pony with little effort, and put my feet in the stirrups. Handed me the reins.

"Wait! No. I can't..."

And they smacked that little Shetland hard on the rump and he took off like a shot.

Ponies are generally pissed off. Maybe they want to be horses. Maybe being cute brings them into contact with too many little kids. In any case that pony didn't like being smacked and he didn't like having this kid on his back. Galloping as hard as possible to dump the kid off seemed to be his plan. I had never galloped like this on anything, which meant pretty plainly to me (though obviously not the counselors) that I didn't know how. Just then the pony noticed the three big horses up ahead and in true pony fashion poured on some extra speed to get to where he hoped to bite one of those suckers on the ass. The big horses, sensibly, didn't think that would be a good idea and we all streaked across the field in front of the assembled camp.

The PA blared out over the campgrounds, "Sidney Glick to the rescue!!"

And I, I was learning something. That was – not falling off seemed more important than the fact that I didn't know how to ride. I grabbed hold of that pony's mane and hung on for dear sweet life. And I discovered that galloping on this little horse didn't only feel terrifying. It felt great. Riding a *little* horse was cool.

Later that week, I went down to the stables thinking I should take the pony out for a ride. It had felt so right on the thing. I felt newly confident about my ability to control a horse *if it was small enough*. I saddled the pony and got on, thinking to walk him a couple times around the corral before taking him out for a glorious run. But that pony again had his issues with control and instead bolted directly across the corral towards the split rail fence. "This stupid pony's got to stop," I surmised, "there's a fence right in front of him." But the pony didn't stop, and cat-like, seemed to know that there was just enough room for him to run full speed under the fence with maybe a 1/2 inch to spare. That meant that the split rail caught me right in the stomach and the next thing I knew I was gasping for breath, on my back on the ground with the fence rail lying broken across my chest and all the stable guys were running toward me laughing and nervous at the same time. And then the summer was over and I hadn't ridden since. Some sixteen, seventeen years since

The following morning Sheila and I are enjoying breakfast.

"Big day today." she says.

"What's that?"

"The horse trader's coming with a horse to show you."

"Yeah, about that. I don't think I'm going to be here long enough to ..."

Helen rushes in.

"He's here!"

"Who?"

"The trader. And what a horse!"

Everyone runs out leaving me.

"Is it small?" I call after them.

★ ★ ★ ★ ★

In the courtyard everyone is gathered around an Afghan man holding a horse by the reins. The horse is cinched up tightly pulling his head up. He is a light grey, almost white, dappled with grey and black, with a black mane and tail and black and white legs and nose. He looks wild and excited. Snorting. A regular sized horse.

I feel the need to say something, "He's not small. And what's the matter with him?"

"Oh," says Helen, "they strap him up tight and probably give him some speed to make him look spirited. But he's a great looking horse."

"I was hoping for a smaller horse." Nobody is listening to me.

"Get on him and give him a try," Helen urges me.

"You know, Helen, Its been so long since I've been on a horse that I'll just be thinking about me on a horse. You know so much more about it. Why don't you give him a try."

"Sure!" She takes the reigns from the trader and jumps on the horse's back. The horse snorts and paces nervously. Helen walks him out the gate and up to the corner. She turns him up the road, pauses, and kicks him off. The horse rears back and seems to hang there for a second like a demon, then leaps off behind the wall. I stand, staring at the spot where the horse was. Moments later they reappear from the other direction. They come flying up and stop. The horse is no less wild looking. Helen is wild looking as well. She jumps off his back.

"What a horse! This is the best horse he's ever brought around!"

"I asked for a small horse."

"He is small," says David.

"How much is he?"

"Let's go inside," says David.

They all go in. I cast nervous glances back at the beast.

Inside tea has been served. David and the trader converse in Farsi. Occasionally David gestures toward me and the trader grunts.

After a while I say, "How much does he want?

"It comes to about two hundred dollars. That's good for a horse of this quality."

"I'll give him a hundred," I say.

"No, no, says David, "you don't want to lose this horse."

Uh huh. "That's it. One hundred dollars and he has to throw in the saddle."

David looks sourly at me. "Let me handle this."

David and the trader converse some more. Eventually things come to a conclusion and they rise from their cushions.

"He's yours," says David.

I find this hard to believe. "For a hundred?"

"Yeah," says David

"Really?"

"He's yours."

I go out to the courtyard where the horse is tied. I walk over to the horse who eyes me nervously.

"Well, looks like its you and me...... Aren't you gonna whinny and nudge me with your nose like a cowboy horse?"

I reach toward the horse who snorts and jerks back. I go back inside. "I think I'm gonna need some time with the horse. Do you know someplace I can rent for a month that'll be good for riding?"

"Paghman," says Helen. "Its a hill town outside Kabul, where the British used to go in the summers. Very nice."

"Yeah I'll find a place up there you can rent," says David. "I'll have the horse delivered there." He speaks some words to the trader who grunts and leaves.

Helen continues to be excited. "This is great! What a horse! You'll really have a time."

"I'm sure." I turn to David. "Well, thanks for that."

"That's what I do," says David, "Fulfiller of dreams."

Yeah.

Paghman

So I rented a house in Paghman, a little village up in the mountains outside of Kabul. It was outside this village where the King kept his country estate. Also, the English had been there, and had used the spot for one of their mountain getaways when the heat and bustle of the city had gotten to be too much for them.

All along the overland routes from Europe, to the far edges of India and beyond, the English had built Victorian summer houses as well as their in-town houses. Some of these cultures had embraced English styles even as they overthrew the Brits themselves. India was like that. They spoke a lot of English there; it was the language of government and the major press. Certain Hindi are always acting the very most proper British role. Other countries, like Afghanistan, had rejected it all. The English language was rarely to be seen, and the people had no desire to emulate the Brits. All that was left of their passing were some lovely Victorian homes.

Trader David had made arrangements for this place, and I arrived having never seen it. The trip to Paghman was by a little bus that was filled to overflowing with the locals. When I say overflowing I mean that quite literally, because the bus was not only full inside, it's roof was completely filled with riders as well. At least twenty people sat up there, holding on to whatever they could. In the next few weeks as I went back and forth between the city and the village I tried occasionally to ride up there, but they always refused my requests. "Not for you silly foreigners," was the sense of what they would say.

Because the Afghans did consider Westerners silly. That was one of the beauties of the place. They had such a self-confidence there. All along the route, in Turkey, in Iran and later in Pakistan, I met people who longed to live like Westerners. Business people in particular, aspired to be just like Westerners, in dress and in what they assumed about our lifestyles. That included greed and power in particular. The Afghan, however, considered his culture to be the only sensible one in the known universe. Foreigners were some level or another of idiot, to mostly be tolerated or ignored, although money could be made from a Westerner, of course. I could see that in certain ways, their control of their women in particular, they had some seriously mistaken ideas, but I admired their sense of self.

Sheila and I are in front of a walled yard on the road just up from the village. The gate swings open and a strange little old man rushes out to hold it. His face is twisted and scarred. He is from the Hazara, a subservient Mongol people from the north.

"This must be Mazur," Sheila says. "Mazur?"

The man nods quickly. His eyes do not meet Sheila's. He rubs his hands together. He doesn't speak.

I say, "Shalom Aleichem, Mazur."

Mazur's eyes dart up for a brief moment and meet mine. He silently mouths, "Aleichem Shalom," and nods.

We walk through the gate. Before us is a large white Victorian house. Surrounding the house are beautiful gardens. I'm surprised and impressed.

"Wow. This is great."

"Yeah."

"Victorians. Everywhere you Brits have been, you've left a slime trail of beautiful Victorian homes."

"This one's been kept in pretty good shape, don't you think?" she says as we go into the open front door.

"Yeah."

We enter into a large front room with a fireplace. A great staircase rises up in the center to the second floor. The room is completely empty of any furnishings.

Sheila explains. "They never use them, the rich Afghans who own them now. They come picnicking in the yard sometimes. That's why there's no furniture. No one ever lives here. They have their own way of sleeping and sitting and shitting, and these old houses don't work for them."

"Empty is OK with me," I say. "Looks spacey this way. It feels like the British, after creating and occupying the place, have become ghosts, dematerializing, with all their possessions."

"Yeah. ... Mazur is the caretaker. But he doesn't take care of you, he takes care of the place. He's doesn't speak much in his native Farsi so he's not going to learn any English. David says if you see a problem point to it and Mazur will take care of it. And he'll take care of the horse. Don't expect much more." We stop in front of a doorway to another room. "These are Mazur's nuts."

She points into the room where the room is filled with hickory nuts in a pile four feet high. Mazur bobs in front of the pile and looks anxiously toward me.

"Yes, "I say nodding to him and then the pile, "these are your nuts. Mazur. A very fine pile of nuts. I imagine this used to be a sitting room." I nod to Mazur who happily nods back. We move on to the kitchen.

Sheila continues the tour. "And running water when you pump this handle." She does it and water flows. "There's another one in the loo. I'm told you can actually have a two minute hot shower with a little effort."

"Really. Deluxe. Thank David again for finding it. You know Sheila, you can stay out here as long as you want."

"Thanks, I know. I'll stay the night, but this is roughing it a bit for me. I'll be better off at Helen's with a scented bath and my nice big bed."

Mazur motions for us to follow him through the kitchen into the stables. He shows us the place he has prepared for the horse.

"Yes, Tashakoor, Mazur. Tashakoor." I thank him sincerely. Mazur nods, pleased.

There is a banging at the gate. Mazur runs to it and opens a portal and looks out. He swings open the gate. It is the horse trader and his boy. The boy holds the reigns of their two horses. The trader holds my horse.

"Shalom Aleichem," I say.

"Aleichem Shalom," says the trader.

I walk around the horse.

"Looks like its got all the hardware. Stirrups, a bit, a blanket. And the belt across his belly."

"The cinch," says Sheila. "Just how long has it been since you've ridden a horse?"

"Well, I was seven so that would be about 17 years ago".

"Well then. Good luck. "

"He still looks kind of demonic," He is pacing in place and snorting.

"Yup. When do you give it a go?"

"No sense puttin it off. Let's find out."

I grab the saddle and try to get my foot up to the stirrup, but it's too high. The trader stops me and shows me how to lengthen them. We lengthen both sides. The trader shows me how to tighten the cinch. He smacks the horse in the belly and the horse sucks it in so the cinch can be pulled tight. I nod. That's it for equestrian school. I grab the saddle with both hands and pull myself awkwardly up. The horse snorts and steps backward nervously. The trader yanks the reigns. Then, holding the bridle he carefully lifts the reins up to me. I get settled and signal him to let go. The horse steps back and begins to turn around. I pull his head forward. The horse stops. I look up the road, breathe a couple times, then give the horse a gentle kick. Again, the horse rears back, frozen for a second...

Uh oh.

...then leaps forward into a crazed gallop up the road.

I feel the beast beneath me. Big, powerful. More powerful than this stupid little thing clinging to his back.. The horse rocks in his gallop, forward and back as we fly up the road. Fly. We are flying up the road. The horse, big and brute, and I, are flying as one. Yoooooooooooooo.

The horse has been dashing madly up the forest trail, past little meadows, past stands of birch, from the dark into the sun. And then, of course, I remember that I don't really know how to ride and I start bumping around in the saddle, pull in the reins and the horse stops.

"OKayyyyy. OK OK OK OK. That was pretty good. Pretty good." I am out of breath as if I had been running myself. I lean over and pat the horse who flinches at the touch but stays in place. I turn him and we walk back down the road.

In the morning Sheila and I come out to the stable. The horse eyes us warily.

"Ready for some breakfast, boy?" I say looking around for his food.

"You know Mazur's been paid to take care of the horse."

"I know, but I'd just as soon do it. I'm hoping Herat will like me more if I give him his food."

"You've named him Herat?"

"Yeah," I say, "after the city of horses."

"Nice."

Mazur comes in but I gesture that I will feed my horse. Mazur nods and brings over water. He shows me the hay and grain and how much to give the horse.

★ ★ ★ ★ ★

I watch the horse eat for a while then follow Sheila into the garden where Mazur is now working. The caretaker goes to the upper section of a little stream at the back of the garden and pulls out a slate which causes the stream to run toward a dry section at the far end of the garden. He puts the slate in the ground at another spot and the stream on this side of the garden stops.

"Look what he's doing," Sheila says.

"He's irrigating the whole garden by rerouting the one little stream."

"With a few flat stones."

"It works."

"It does indeed.," she says. ... "I'm going. There's a Kabul bus in the village in a half hour."

"I'll walk you."

"No, thanks, I like to walk down the street alone in the daytime. I feel like its my duty."

"Your duty?"

"To the women," she says, "They should see a woman walk the streets like a real person, in beautiful colors, with her face showing."

"Well, remember, you are a painted Western whore."

"My body is fully covered at all times."

"Still, very noticeable."

"I'll always be noticeable."

"Notable," I say and kiss her goodbye.

★★★★★

I am riding up a lightly wooded hill. We walk for a while, then Herat stops to eat a choice clump of weeds. I let him for a moment, then pull his head up and we move on. The road we are on is a dirt trail. We come out of the trees and there is an open stretch. I kick Herat off. He rears as he always does and takes off at a gallop up the road. I cling comfortably. As we run Herat begins to drift from right to left across the road. I pull him straight with difficulty. We stop.

"Why do you always do that? You fade left and run off the road."

The horse puts his head down and begins to eat.

"Yes. Eat. I understand. You want two things. Eat, and go home and eat." I walk him over to where a view has opened up.

"Look. A view. A beautiful view. Aren't you going to whinny and make huffing sounds? No? Well, its a privilege just to be up here. And a privilege to be here with my horse, who will not speak."

Herat huffs as he eats.

★★★★★

Further up the hill we come to a meadow. There is a space like an open amphitheater.

"Look at this. What a place for a rock show." Herat eats. "Put the band over there. Cook up some food over there."

I get down and tie Herat's reins to a sapling. He chews the vegetation around him.

"If you could charter a flight cheap enough. You could fly sixty to a hundred people out to Kabul from London, put them up in Kabul for the weekend and bus them up here for a concert. Give a couple great bands a free weekend trip to Afghanistan so they'll play for free. Wish somebody would offer something like that to me. ... Could happen. Sixty people at a hundred pounds is six thousand pounds. About fifteen thousand dollars. Could happen." I rub my ass. "Did you know that your saddle is basically wood? That's gonna take some getting used to. You've got a blanket between you and the wood saddle. Hey, maybe I should sit on my jacket." I put the jacket on the saddle and sit on it. "Yeah. That's better. Thanks for the tip, Boy." We begin to ride off. "Riding the horse, OK"

The horse breaks into its trot. I bounce in the saddle, slamming my bottom. "Except for the fucking trot!" I nudge the horse into the gallop and things smooth out. Then the horse drops into something like a canter.

"Ooooooooooooooooooo. That's good."

The horse descends through the trot again with me bouncing and then back to a walk.

"We're gettin there." I pat the horse's neck.

Travelers found their way to my house. First I had friends over. Dave and Barry came by for a few days, but they really preferred to lie on their beds at a hotel in the middle of the Kabul action. Being in the city meant that you were in the midst of the flow of travelers, an ever-unfolding storybook of road tales. A cuppa tea, a fine Afghani joint, and a good laugh about somebody's misadventures, that is one of the high arts of the traveler.

Once word started getting around, the trickle of travelers to my door increased. I'd let them stay a night, and invite the ones I enjoyed to stay on longer. Nobody was there for more than three or four days. Most were moving, flowing toward India or back.

Women were not scarce on the road. Most of them were part of traveling couples. That's a good way to travel not only for the support and security, but also for the sharing. The solitary traveler when coming upon a stupendous sight will often wish that he could be sharing this moment with someone simpatico. Look at the sight, look at each other, and something is shared, known, never to be known in this exact way by anyone else.

But in addition, there was a steady stream of women traveling on their own. Every one of these women had an inner strength that had brought her this far. For every reason that a man had to keep his eyes open on the road, these women had twenty. The routes of travelers are determined as much by the congeniality of the countries they are passing through as by their geography. Each traveler takes a leap of faith that he will carry the protection of the worldwide code of safe passage. That it is in the interests of the local country to not fuck with the ability of the world to safely pass through. But there is violence everywhere, and in many of these countries there is an implicit belief that by being a woman on your own, you are announcing your immorality and your availability. That you're asking for it.

So for everyone, but women especially, that meant being aware of the situations they were getting themselves into, and trying, though independent, to never be alone.

I wake up in my sleeping bag in front of the big fireplace. It's November and cold in the nights. Each night I feed the fire until I fall asleep and get it going again in the morning. Sleeping on the floor is not a problem as long as I have a pillow, and I can always fashion one out of my extra clothes. I throw some small pieces of wood on the fire and it flares up. I pump water into a small metal saucepan and put it on the fire. I open three canisters and spoon out three powders into a cup, one at a time.

"Coffee (instant) ....powdered milk.....and sugar."

I lift the saucepan off the fire and pour the boiling water into the mix, and stir it. I drink.

"Ahh – Coffee! Delicious."

I sit satisfied, occasionally sipping. There is a sudden knocking at the gate outside. I go out and swing it open. There is a young American woman there. Pretty with stringy blond hair.

"Are you Les?"

"Yeah."

"I'm Susan. I heard you let people stay here a couple days if they ask nice."

"That's nice enough. Come on in."

Susan was a bit of a hard case. That had been her defense along the way. Take no shit. Give shit where necessary. Like so many women travelers she was pretty. OK, lets say a word about this. I keep saying this one was pretty, that one was pretty. Were they all pretty? They mostly were. And I found more women pretty than other men did. I felt that a lot of a woman's attraction rises from her spirit. It shows on the surface in her eyes and her smile. Many women had captured my heart, in a moment, with a look and a smile. These women out there were strong. Their spirits were strong and obvious. That made my heart flutter.

"This is very cool," says Susan. The emptiness of the place made the Victorian detail stand out.

"Yeah. Come on upstairs and you can pick out a bedroom."

Upstairs we walk from room to empty room.

"They're all pretty much the same," I say, "no beds."

"Where do you sleep?"

"Down at the end here... unless I'm crashing in front of the fireplace." We go into the room at the end of the hallway. It is large and bright but holds nothing but a pack. "Pretty much like the rest."

"I'll sleep here, with you. All right?"

"All right."

Susan pokes her head through the next doorway.

"A toilet!"

"Yeah. You have to throw a bucket of water into it to make it work but you get to sit down."

"What's this?" She reaches up to a brass contraption on a high shelf.

"Oh yeah. You fill this part with water, and you make a little fire down here in this lower section, and you," .

"..get a little shower. A hot shower." She turns to me, grabs my shirt and pulls me to her. She gives me a long kiss on the mouth. "I'm gonna take a shower. Wait for me in our bedroom. I'm gonna come down...and fuck the shit out of you."

"You know, you don't have to do that to stay here.."

"Yes or no?"

"Yes Mam."

I need to change some money so I go down to the little bank in the village. I walk into a standard mud commercial space, with a painted Farsi sign and four block letters that say BANK. BANK and BUS are the only English words in the village. It is a large drear room with several desks. At each sits a man in a white shirt, leaning over a pile of paper work. There are no women. One man rises and comes over to me.

"Hello. Hello. You have come to change some monies?" It is my friend. Bank Manager 3.

"Yes. Nice to see you again. Shalome Alechem. Here's that nickel I said I would bring you." I give him the American coin. It is exotic to him with its indian and buffalo. I say, "One traveler's check. Twenty dollars. American express, OK?"

"Yes. Barkley's Bank and American Express. Both are very good. We can change."

"Thanks. Tashakoor."

I bow slightly to the teller who smiles and bows back. The teller makes some notes from my passport and counts out the money.

Bank manager 3 says, "I was also thinking to ask if there are some possibilities that you would come one night to eat an evening meal at my home."

"Yes, thank you. I would like that. I have never been inside an Afghan home. I would be very happy to come and eat with you."

"Please come tomorrow. Meet me one street down from the bank at 4:30 in the afternoon. OK?"

"Yes. Tomorrow. 4:30. OK."

The next morning I walk down the hill through the village. I stop in front of the yoghurt man. The yoghurt man has a big clay bowl full of yoghurt and he scoops a cup of yoghurt into bowls that people hand him. Next to him is a stand where a man sells strawberries. Further down, I stop in front of the meat man. I point to half a butchered goat hanging behind the man.

"In two days....(I point to the sun and mime the sun passing through the sky twice) Two days I come here for one whole goat..all of goat. Two days OK?"

The man points to the goat and asks a question.

"Yes. One goat. Tomorrow and tomorrow."

The man says yes and nods.

I walk over to a wooden table where an old man is cooking over a wood fire. I point to a pile of eggs nicely stacked into a pyramid.

"Two eggs please. Fried?" I mime frying. If people expect to understand you they usually will. If they think they're not going to understand you, sometimes they won't even if you're speaking their own language.

The old man nods to say he has it.

"Nan?" he asks.

"Yes. Nan."

The old man opens a chest and pulls out a ball of dough which he flattens with his hands. He opens the door in the top of something like a bee hive oven, and then, slings the dough up against the inside of the fiery oven, and closes the door. A boy comes over and gives me a glass with a pile of sugar on the bottom, and a pot of tea. He pours my first cup without stirring up the sugar. The old man puts a scoop of orange lamb fat into a brass bowl and sets it over the fire. When it is hot and clear and boiling he cracks two eggs in, waits, then scoops them out and puts them on a plate. (Don't ask for a scrambled egg. He'll scramble it with all the lamb fat.) He opens the door of the oven and reaches in with a poker-like implement and pulls out the fully baked flat bread. The boy brings them to the table.

"Tashakoor." I poke an egg. The yolk runs out. "Perfect." I push some egg up onto the hot bread and take a bite.

"Ummmm. No. That's perfect." The boy walks over with a crock of jam.

"Jem?"

"No. That's perfect"

"No jem?"

"Yes. Tashakoor. I will take the jam. Everything is good, perfect. Yes, yes, yes."

But the major food that I ate every day in Afghanistan was lamb kebobs. As I have mentioned, the entire country smells always from the kebobs being grilled over small wood fires. Maybe it's the meat. Maybe it's the wood they burn, but it was like the whole culture had decided to put on a scent. A countrywide incense. It was heady and beautiful. In 1970, Afghanistan smelled of woodsmoke and barbecue.

KippyCom

Dear L -

Maybe you heard, I tried to call you yesterday, not really thinking you'd be anywhere reachable, but hoping you'd get a message eventually.

Last week I went tripping down memory lane as I prepared my trunk for leaving. I'm stepping into matrimony on December 9. Wish you'd been around to talk to. None of this is easy – probably not even good or necessary, but you know how I tend to plow into furrows of mediocrity. For shame. Anyway, I wanted you to know because I care about you and don't want to lose touch with you.

I dared to reread a few of your old letters. No crushing them to my concave breasts; just a simple reading. They were all you – alive and warm. One was about Eastern music and Andy.

If you hear about any exceptional jobs for me (ie. with Woody Allen or Lester Lanin) let me know.

Be a good boy, sing a song for me, and don't chastise me too severely. This is only Chapter three. I wish (ideally) it were you.

Love and don't be remote – Kippy

Later I come walking up the street. The bank manager steps out to greet me, a little furtive. Maybe he shouldn't be doing this.

"Yes, yes. Come. This way."

He leads me down to a little side street. We enter a small court-yard through a gate in a mud wall. He opens the door and he is greeted by a woman who takes his things.

Although she is not wearing the burka all the women wear on the street, she is completely covered with all but her eyes hidden in scarves. The man speaks to her but she does not speak in front of me. The bank manager and I take off our shoes and go into a room where there are wide cushions on the floor and a low table. The walls are bare except for a framed picture of the King on the wall. We sit. The wife comes in with tea. The bank manager speaks to her. She nods to him, but still does not speak. She brings in a bowl of stewed lamb and potatoes with nan for each of us and disappears. It's a little greasy but I eat appreciatively.

"You like Afghani food?" he asks me.

"Yes. Especially the kabobs."

"Yes they are very good."

We eat. The woman does not join us. At the end she returns to clear away the plates.

"You would like some hashish?" asks Bank Manager 3.

This is a surprise. "Yes, very much. You smoke hashish?"

"Oh, yes," he says. He steps out and returns with a water pipe. He puts a piece of charcoal in the top and lights it. When that is lit he crushes some hash on top and offers the mouthpiece to me. I take a deep pull and pass it to the bank manager who takes a deep breath but does not hold it in as long. He exhales and speaks.

"My bosses at the bank know I am a hashish smoker. Because of that, I can never rise higher than bank manager number three, which I am. But, I am happy to be bank manager number three and smoke hashish. Don't you think?"

"I do. In America if bank manager three tells his boss he is smoking hashish at home, he will be fired and probably end up in jail."

"No, that is not good. But you know that in America you can drink alcohol. This we can not do. Here, I would be fired very quickly for that. But who is right?"

"Probably nobody," I say, "but right now...this seems pretty right to me." I take another big hit. "You have invited me into your home. Thank you very much for that. May I ask you some things about your life in Afghanistan?"

"Yes."

"Your wife does not speak to me."

"That would be improper. To speak to a man from ... outside. You are our guest, but of course, you are from the outside."

"So your women wear the burka to limit their ...contact with men? Yes?"

"Yes. Even talking to you would be improper. For a woman to act improperly would be a dishonor. "

"She would dishonor herself by talking to me?"

"She would dishonor her family. Me.

"When that happens, what does an Afghani man do?"

"He must punish her. If the dishonor is great, it could be very very bad."

"She could be killed."

"If the dishonor is great. A woman who dishonors her family is a stain on that family. It could not be left like this."

"Who would kill her?"

"Her husband or her brothers, or her father. Or she could be stoned by the whole village."

"Do you think that's right?"

"Right? Yes. That's the way it has always been."

"I carry a message from young people in America to you and all of your friends. Would you like to hear it?"

"Yes, of course."

"Afghanistan is a country where I see much nobility. People wishing to do right. Honor is a big part of that here. I see that every day. But it does no one honor to oppress, to hold down or injure his brother or his sister. Although things have been done one way for years, that does not make them right. And as my cousin Bob says – the times they are a-changin."

"Yes," says Bank Manager 3, "America is always changing. But here in Afghanistan things change very slowly."

"Get ready."

My goat party. I had sent word to town to tell Barry and Dave, and Sheila and David and Helen, and anyone else that seemed right and all their friends. I had a big barbecue oven type structure in the back yard with a spit so I had decided on roasting a goat. Not that I had ever roasted a goat before. It just sounded good. The morning of the party I walked down to the meat man I had spoken with, and the meat man had the back half of a goat waiting. "Its fine. Plenty for you," he indicated with his hands. "OK." I paid and had him send it up to the house. The meat man knew where I lived. It was a village. Everyone in town knew where everyone lived. Then I went and bought a big bag of very large and fresh strawberries. Then over to the yogurt man. The big clay bowl is close to full.

"Salam. How much for all?" I mime as I speak.

The yogurt man tells me how much for a cup full.

"No. I want all."

"All?" We are continuing to speak with our hands.

"Yes, and the bowl too." I indicate his whole supply. It is maybe a three gallon bowl and only one cup has been scooped out. He comes up with a fair price and I agree. The man seems a little surprised but gives it to me, bowl and all. I expect that this will be considered a big sale and he will be happy, but I can see that now this man's whole day has been thrown off because he no longer has his reason for sitting in his place. Sorry.

Back at the house I build a fire in the barbecue and let it burn for a while to develop some coals. I rub the goat with salt, and with the help of a friend, get it onto a spit and up over the fire. We turn it occasionally by hand. This is gonna take a while. Over the next couple hours people start to arrive. Soon the yard is filled with young men and women. There are several guitars, lots of smoke and the smell of roasting meat. No booze. There isn't any available and nobody seems to notice the lack of it.

Mazur had been frightened away by the provocatively dressed women. We were in a walled compound now and they were ready to let their hair down. Tops too. A couple of women lay sunbathing on a blanket on their backs with their breasts exposed. I saw Mazur peeking around a corner at them. Then he disappeared, not to be seen again that day. Nobody pumped any water for the toilet which made a Texas girl say that I should fire Mazur if he ever did come back. Some guys picked up a piece of wood to chop up for the fire, not noticing that it was an ornamental edge on Mazur's walkway. I rescued it but I could see how distant these cultures were from each other.

The goat was taking a long time to cook. Everyone kept going over to it and poking it. Eventually people began picking little bits off it as the outside cooked. Then suddenly everyone was yanking pieces off it, sometimes half cooked, and that's the way it slowly disappeared over the course of the day. It seemed irresistible and I got a quick course that day in the power of meat. Later, after dark, we sat around a fire and sang Crosby, Stills, Nash, and Young, and Beatles songs into the clear and starry Afghan night.

A few days later a young British man, a friend of Sheila's, arrived at the house with two very elegant and beautiful women, one English one French, on their way to a retreat in India. They were a triple. The women treated him like a prince, and he treated each of them like a princess. He seemed like a very nice guy. There was no chance of these women taking on any other lovers, they were bound into this very lovely group. They moved into one of the large bedrooms and in a few moments had hung silks that immediately transformed the space into a room at an Eastern palace. I sat with them having tea and had to admire their lives. Not only was this guy very very lucky, but each of the women was so obviously loved by the other that they seemed equally blessed. They were a lot like the French people I had met on the beach at Saintes Marie de la Mere **(LUCKY MONKEY IN EUROPE)** How long can something like that work? It's a delicate balancing act to be sure, but what isn't? and these folk made it work then. A couple days later they moved on.

I took a bus into Kabul. I wanted to go to the market. Market places everywhere were usually my favorite part of the town. Not only can the acquisitive buy themselves art, trinkets and food, the entire local culture is displayed, its insides out. The internal workings of a country are better understood when its implements are laid out before you. Do they look functional? Do they have tools for every function we in America find important? Are there tools for functions unknown? What's this thing? Ask them. You don't speak Farsi? Lift up the tool. Inquire with your eyes and hands. They are merchants. It is in their interests to understand you. Most will respond. The man picks up the slender iron hook and mimes reaching up to grab at something. What could he be grabbing? He mimes bringing food to his mouth. "Nan," He says. Nan! It's that tool for grabbing the bread out of the oven. You examine it. The iron has been twisted and worked in a way that is unnecessarily beautiful. It has been made by not just a craftsman, but by an artist. Now you know something more about the place.

Next section of the market you can see layers of clothing you don't get to see on the street. What goes under what. The shirts beneath the jackets. Their socks. Those big colorful socks with the leather bottoms came from Afghanistan. They're in the stalls. Good ones.

Sheila was bringing me to the big market across the river. The Souk. She knew all about the markets from Helen and David, and she knew what I wanted.

"I think its over this way," she is saying. "They think of it as food for the cattle."

'It' was the rest of the marijuana, left behind after the resin had been taken for hash. Nothing was ever smoked out there but the hash itself. Why bother.

"Why do you want this?"

"The hash is so powerful, sometimes just the smell of it makes my teeth rattle. And everyone's always sticking a joint in your mouth."

"Poor boy. "

"Yah. But a couple of days ago I saw a man on the street with a bundle of what looked like marijuana leaf, and it was. I bought a handful of it to try it out and it was good but much mellower than the hash. Nice change."

"Here it is," she says.

A man stands in front of a wagon piled high with, sure enough, marijuana, in bundles.

"How much? "I ask, pointing to a good sized bundle.

The man speaks. I look at Sheila. "That would be … about eleven cents?"

"That's right, dear. "

"Yes," I am saying. "Yes."

We spent the rest of the morning wandering the market, eating and having tea. Sheila was attracted to cloth and clothing, I liked hardware, unusual devices, musical instruments. Sheila was in a stall trying on vests when I noticed something in the next stall. It looked like a small piano keyboard. At first I thought it was some sort of accordion. I pointed to it. The merchant lifted it down from the shelf. He took a cloth and wiped it carefully. He undid a latch on the back and it opened. He pressed it shut again and held down a key…HRRRUMMMMMM. It was a harmonium. Like a little mini organ in a box. Playing long sustained notes and polyphonic chords when more than one key was held down. What a beautiful sound.

Sheila is at my elbow. "You have to have it."

"How much?" I ask.

The man names a price.

"How much?" Sheila is incredulous. Merchant to merchant. He says the price again. She smirks at him and names a price about a quarter of what he has said. He is shocked. He comes down a little. She repeats her price. He comes down halfway and makes motions to wrap it for her. She repeats her price. He begins to whine, to point out what a stunning loss this would be for him. How he would risk losing his business if he has to sell his best things for prices like that. She repeats her price once more and turns to leave. "Yeah yeah," he caves.

"I bought it? "I ask her."

"No. I bought it," she says, and she hands it to me as a present. Sweet girl.

One evening Mazur came to fetch me. Someone was at the gate. It was Bank Manager 3.

"Yes. Hello. Come in," I say

"Oh, no," says Bank Manager 3, "I have just come to ask..."

He has something on his mind, and although he wants to say it, he can't get the words out. He shuffles around, his eyes meeting mine then dropping away.

"Yes? "I encourage him.

"Can I ....? "

"Yes?"

"I would like...."

"Yes??? "

"Can I have one of your women?" asks Bank Manager 3.

I stare at him.

"You have so many and... "

"No."

"But you have..."

"They are not mine." I shake my head and stand back from the gate. The bank manager looks at me a last time then turns and slouches away.

About halfway through my stay in Paghman I decided I needed a couple of buckets to carry food and water for Herat. I had seen some for sale in the village. I rarely took Herat into the village because it made him very nervous. He was high strung anyway but what really made him skittish were the local kids. For some reason they were compulsively drawn to throw rocks at the horse. Maybe it was because I was a foreigner, maybe it was something they commonly did, but whenever I rode past a kid, the kid would bend over, pick up a small stone and throw it at the horse. Not at me. I was never hit and no one ever threw a rock at me when I was walking alone, but when I was on the horse it was somehow irresistible. They wanted to spook the horse. That was the game. Herat had learned this as well, and he viewed small boys with fear.

On this day though, I had decided that it would be easier to bring the buckets back, one strapped on each side of the horse, so I had ridden Herat into the village and down to the bucket man. All the way down the horse had been on edge, his ears flicking around to listen for trouble, his eyes wide. On several occasions young boys had come running up with stones hidden behind them but I had fixed them with a steady glare and they had held back. I got to the shop, dismounted, picked out a couple of appropriate buckets, bought them, and tied them, one on each side, behind my saddle. Then I got on Herat and slowly rode back up through the town.

Between the ever-present boys and the buckets occasionally bumping against his sides, Herat was more nervous than ever. He wanted to walk faster and faster, but whenever he sped up the buckets began to bump and I could see that this could become a problem. But I kept the horse under control and made it back up the road to my gate. I got down and opened it. As he was being led in though, the horse got spooked by something (or nothing) and bolted into the yard. I still held him but as Herat stopped, the buckets came flying into his sides with a bang and he took off, his reigns pulling out of my hands. He began to run madly round and round the gardens and each time he slowed the buckets would slam him again and he would be off. This went on for a while. When I was finally able to get hold of his reins and bring him to a halt, I saw that Herat had destroyed several parts of Mazur's gardens. Mazur, who had come running out, looked at the destruction and groaned. I felt terrible.

During this period I went into Kabul to see if I could find some official way to ride my horse through the Khyber Pass, which also meant out of Afghanistan, into Pakistan. I was sure there would be some bureaucratic bullshit about it, and figured I was better off getting it settled here in Kabul, than working it out at the border.

I had decided that over the border was the only direction I could ride because it continued my travels. If I were going to be true to the vision I had constructed for Sheila, or rather the vision I had cobbled together in front of Sheila, of acclimating myself slowly to the local bacteria I would have to continue moving forward on my journey. I could take a trip for a week or so up into the mountains, but to start and stop in Kabul would just be hanging out on a horse. Not the same thing. To act out this little fantasy I would have to travel, to end up somewhere else. That meant up into the mountains, through the Khyber Pass, and down into Pakistan in the Indus Valley. The Indian subcontinent. That would be far enough. The next continent.

The Khyber Pass. A magical name. You could do worse in your travels than to go from place to place because of their magical names. There was usually some real reason for a place's fame. Probably something big happened there. Sometimes it was a battle. Sometimes it was a confluence of rivers and roads. Sometimes it was a culture in full blossom. The Khyber Pass is a narrow passage way up in the mountains, on the main trail from Europe to India. Everything changes here. All across Turkey and Persia the people have basically the same features as Europeans. In Pakistan and India they don't. Europe and India. Two huge genetic pools held in place by topography, where the difficult and remote Khyber Pass is the best overland route for passing goods, ideas and genes.

Each trading caravan and each army eventually had to go up into these mountains where a trail had been made. Here you could often move with only three or four abreast, and where most of the time a hundred foot cliff rises on one side of the road, and a hundred foot drop falls off the other. And in these mountains live tribes of mountain people. Because of their location, neither country they border could ever control these tribes. This is their turf. And they have been fierce and merciless keeping it theirs. They've stopped many armies here including the British. Whole armies destroyed. And because their control was complete in this border area, the tribes specialized in the movement of goods from one side to the other. Smuggling. It was their business. And is today. (And this is where Bin Laden went to hide.)

I went to the municipal building in Kabul. As in most of the world, this meant waiting in a grey room to get into a similar room where someone at a desk wished he was elsewhere. Following suggestions I had found my way to this building to speak to a man who had been described as the President of Customs. He sent me on to a man they called the Minister of Trade. Was it really the Afghan Minister of Trade? Well, I was in Kabul and as an American I was possibly rich and brought the possibilities of baksheesh.

"Ah. Hello," said the Minister.

"Hello," I answered brightly.

Baksheesh is not generally hidden away like a Western bribe. Normally you'll ask how much baksheesh is needed. The right man will tell you how much backsheesh will be needed to pay, not only him, but everyone who will have anything to do with getting your job done. You can pay, negotiate or walk away, but some baksheesh is due. Often the baksheesh is the only money involved. Some service for some baksheesh. Its gonna be there. For instance, if you wanted something that required filling out a form, you could go and do that but without baksheesh that form will never move from desk to desk. So I was there to try to buy my way out of the country.

"And what can I do for you?"

"I own a horse and I will be traveling with him to Peshawar."

"Peshawar? Peshawar is Pakistan."

"Yes I want to ride my horse to Peshawar, Pakistan."

"But the road to Peshawar goes through the Khyber Pass. No one controls the Khyber Pass. You can not ride a horse through there."

"People go through the pass every day."

"Yes in a bus or a car, yes. And they do not stop. You can not go through on a horse. And anyway, there is an Afghan law that says no foreigner can take our horses out of the country.

This goes back to the Bushkazi. Polo with a dead goat. One rider will scoop it up with a stick and gallop down the field while the other team tries to beat the shit out of him. They smack him with their sticks and crash their horses together. Very exciting with great riding and with horses bred to be fast, brave, and a little crazy. As a result there are very fine horses in Afghanistan. Naturally the British tried to take all the best, so when the Brits got bounced, a law was put in place to forbid any more horses being taken out of the country. That is, by foreigners. Local people from both countries, and nomadic tribes in the area crossed the border on horses all the time. I figured I could work it out with baksheesh.

"Yes. I've heard of that law but I thought maybe there was some way."

'No! You can't go," said the Minister jumping up. 'You will be shot and killed. They will shoot you for your horse."

Oh man, this guy is really playing this up, I thought. This is gonna be expensive.

"Maybe you could help me talk to the right people... Maybe there's some kind of permit I could buy....?" I began so we could move directly into pricing.

"There are no right people. There is no permit. Good bye." I wasn't going be profitable to him, he had realized. Just another stupid foreigner.

"I could.... "

"No. Good bye." The man got up and left the room. Shit. Well, I'll deal with this at the border.

Barry and Dave turned up at the house during my last week there.

"We're headed for Pakistan," Barry said. "Leaving tomorrow. We figured we'd meet up with you there in Peshawar."

"To Peshawar!" ...we all said and clinked our tea glasses.

"I brought you something. For your ride." Dave held up a really nice capey thing. "I've seen the riders out here wearing them."

"Great," I said. "I'll try it out."

One of my last chores before leaving Paghman was mailing home the harmonium. I couldn't carry it on the horse, I already had my guitar. And also I had discovered that if you disassembled the whole thing, there was a space inside just big enough to accommodate a tupperware tub filled with the Afghan grass. I cleaned it all down, packed it tight, and threw in a couple good-sized hunks of hash. Then I glued the harmonium together so it couldn't be easily opened and when I was done it still played. I wrapped it all carefully and took it down to the village post office and mailed it off. But I hadn't paid anyone baksheesh so I never saw it again.

A couple days before I was planning to leave, I was walking up from a chi shop in Paghman when I saw an odd looking vehicle parked on the side of the road. There were a couple of Westerners standing around it and when I got close I could see that on the side below some violet tinted windows it said BRITISH EXPEDITION-ARY GROUP.

"Scuse us," said one of the men. "Do you speak English?" He was clearly British.

"In a way."

"Good. Good," a more officious looking one said.. "We are the British Expeditionary Group, on our way to India. We're headed for Kabul but right now we are having some kind of a problem with our truck. One of these local fellows said there was an American with a house nearby where we might stay the night."

"That would probably be me. No problem. It's about a mile up the road. What about your truck?"

"Oh, Richard will take care of the truck." He looked disdainfully toward the fellow who had first haled me.

"Yeah," said Richard. "I'll have it fixed in about an hour. Just get these folks settled. (And out of his hair, it seemed.) and I'll be up in a bit."

A total of six more people, men and women, came out of the truck and grumbled as I led them up the road. The leader John spoke continually...

"Yes, we're traveling from London to New Delhi in a vehicle outfitted for any eventuality and the complete comfort of our client/explorers. Fine trip, fine trip. Getting a chance to see lots of fine sights along the way. Many different cultures, Colorful costumes. Lots of odd things to eat. Eh?"

He looked toward his group but they were not responsive.

"Well, it not too hot today is it Mr. Warrik?"

Mr. Warrik gave him a dirty look. I opened the gate.

"Well look at this," said John.

Here was a touch of England for them in the middle of this ungodly place, a stately Victorian with all the comforts of.... No this place was completely empty. Forget beds, this place had no chairs.

"Yes, well, we'll make do just fine in here." He spoke, looking around nervously. "Just fine, fine."

A while later I was showing them how to make tea in the fire-place when Richard came driving up with the truck. John and the passengers grabbed their sleeping bags and ran off to claim their spots. Richard and I were left alone.

"Refreshment?" I said holding up a joint.

"Absafuckinlutely," responded Richard.

We retired to the garden. Richard (Palmer), it turned out was a professional rock and roll roadie, having traveled with many of the most famous British bands. On a whim he had accepted this job as mechanic with the British Expeditionary Group, where he would be paid to take a trip out to India. Sounded good, but early on in the trip it had become clear to the 'clients' that the ride was longer, more mo-notonous and harder than they had envisioned. Many of the Expedi-tion's promises went unfulfilled and on top of all that, almost every couple (they were mostly couples) were in some stage or another of deterioration or downright demolition. John, their leader, was a major asshole. In fact, he had organized and planned the trip with his girl-friend Jill. But then he had fallen in love with a different Jill, who was now traveling with him. But Jill #1 had decided that she wasn't going to forfeit her trip because of those two jerks so she was in the truck too. John could be counted on to make every bad decision at every opportunity. Richard had found himself on his own, talking to him-self, ignoring the others and working continually on a vehicle that seemed to have been designed for every possible condition except motoring down the hot dry highway. They had six more weeks to go.

"Then you'll need this. I can't take it with me," I said and handed him my bag of grass with a big lump of hash.

"Yesssss," said Richard.

And we became friends for life.

I Take Off

The house rental was coming to an end and that meant it was time to begin the ride. I was glad to have a clear deadline. I work best with deadlines. After tomorrow I would have no place to sleep and no stable for my horse. On the road. As mentioned before, I loved the moment of departure, especially if I didn't know where I would sleep at the end of the day. Casting off.

On my last full day two German couples arrived in a flashy car they had driven from Germany. They were all attractive, in their late twenties, early thirties. They had a whiff of the bourgeoisie about them but they were nice. They had heard about me and the place, and were there to see what it would take to arrange for a night's lodging. They assumed they would have to pay.

"What a nice place," the women were saying.

"You have rooms?" said one of the guys.

"Sure. Go upstairs and pick any room you like. I'm sleeping down here." I pointed to my spot in front of the fireplace.

"OK. Sure. Good," he said and they went upstairs to have a look, wondering, I could tell, how much it would cost.

When they came down I was trying to figure out how to deal with my pack. It's large lightweight metal infrastructure had been perfect for walking and throwing in cars and busses up till now but it clearly was not going to work on the horse. Anyway, I had solved the problem of how to carry my things by getting a pair of saddlebags. They were like two big flat bags (made of heavy tapestry) sewn together flap to flap, that were slung over the horse behind the saddle. So I had no need for my pack as long as I was on the horse. After that would take care of itself. The German guys noticed the pack.

"We have nossing like this at home," said the one I'll call Hans, admiring the new high tech construction.

"No," said Franz, "Not like this one." Then... "We can give you 500 afs for two rooms," said Hans. (About six dollars.) "They have no beds." Possibly this was news to me.

"No. I'm sorry. I can't do that," I said, "I'll take nothing for the rooms and you have to take this pack." This caused a real problem. Everyone assumed a language derailment.

"No. No," said Franz "500 afs. There are no beds, too!" He looked around for affirmation but Hans was just as confused. The women had started to smirk.

"No," I said, "I have to insist. The price has to be nothing and if you don't agree to take the pack you'll have to leave right now." The men were completely baffled.

"OK. OK," said one of the women. "But you are a hard bargainer."

"Yes I am," I agreed.

★ ★ ★ ★ ★

It was the last evening and I went out to feed Herat. I had fed him every day, brought him water and grain and hay because I wanted the horse to like me. It sort of worked. Mazur would have fed him in return for all the valuable manure he was getting for free. I could sense in the beginning that Mazur was a little concerned that I might object to his taking all that fine shit, but I had shown him it was all right. Mazur knew today was my last day and he was there to .... say something non-verbal. I appreciated it. I had come prepared. I took out two thousand afs. (About 22 dollars). "Tashakur," I said, and held it out to him. "Thank you." The old caretaker didn't seem to understand. "For you," I said. "Baksheesh," and gave him the money. He took it and stared at it. I understood. He was so low in the order of things in his society that he rarely got the opportunity for baksheesh, and nobody gets *two thousand afs*. "For the garden, then," I said and pointed to where he had been repairing the damage Herat had done. He nodded and smiled. "Tashakur," he almost said. "Tashakur."

Back in the house I reread a note from Sheila that she had left a few days before.

"Just felt right to leave Paghman as peacefully and silently as the first time I found her.

You are truly a special person – and I love you down to the ground – and back up again. And I'm glad, glad, glad for the time spent with you. More than anything that I wanted to stay need not be said.

I'll be in Delhi around Christmas, London in the spring at Mothers in Sudberry. What a lot of nonsense.

God Bless

Take Care – Sheila

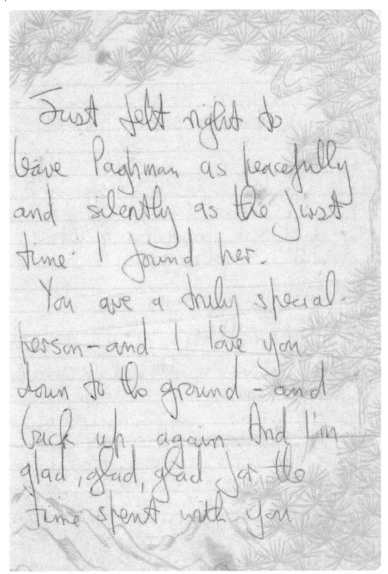

Just felt right to leave Paghman as peacefully and silently as the first time I found her.

You are a truly special person - and I love you down to the ground - and back up again. And I'm glad, glad, glad of the time spent with you

The next morning I fed Herat for the last time in the stable. He was going to carry some hay and grain in one of the bags. I was carrying water for myself in my canteens. I usually drank tea whenever I could because the water was boiled. (Maybe.) Out on the road I was going to drop in a pill that killed all the bacteria each time I filled my canteen. I'd brought these from home. Mazur turned up and I showed him I was leaving behind the two new buckets. Yes. Good.

When Herat was done eating I began to saddle him, but Mazur wanted to do it for me. OK. I went back for a last check on the house. I wanted to be sure it was empty and clean. I went upstairs, room to room. Once more everything was empty. Just the nuts in the sitting room. I had been there and like the British I would be gone. Just another ghost. Just a story told by the yogurt man.

Mazur had saddled Herat but he had left the bags to me. We got them up on the horse. Herat wasn't sure he liked them. "Easy boy." I hoisted up my guitar and tied it to the saddlebag on the right side. It didn't look too good.

I had put the guitar on the right because I got on from the left, but when I tried to swing my leg up over the saddle the guitar still got in the way and Mazur had to hold the horse tightly while I finally got myself situated. Precariously situated. I walked the horse out the open gate and started down the hill. I decided that waving to Mazur might spook the horse so I didn't. I'm sure he understood.

We rode down first through the little village. As usual boys accumulated and I had to keep a tight lid on them with my eyes. We reached the end of the village and got on the road to Kabul. As we started to make our way down toward the city, Herat began to take every opportunity to try to turn around. *Go back to the stable. Eat.* I kept us going down the road. As each mile away from home accrued the horse was becoming more and more frantic. *Go Home! Eat! Why are we going so far from the stable?!* The road came out to a promontory. I saw the city below.

Suddenly Herat reared up and yelled. I clung to his back. The guitar fell to the ground. The ground almost beneath the horse's hooves. I jumped off and pulled him away.

I tied Herat to a tree and went over to pick up my guitar. I unzipped the case and pulled it out. Turned it over ...and.... it was OK. But this wasn't going to work. The guitar couldn't – shouldn't be on this ride.

I temporarily tied it back in place. Then I took the horse by the bridle and we walked a mile down the road. Then another, then another. When I got back on, maybe five miles down the road, the horse had given up. Home was gone. We were traveling.

★ ★ ★ ★ ★

A while later we came into Kabul. From here I led the horse. I was crossing the city to get to the hotel where Dave and Barry had stayed. By now it was early afternoon. I knew that I had to get out of the city before dark to find a place to stay with the horse. And it was better that way. Get going. Out onto the road. But I had to solve this problem of the guitar. I found my way to their hotel and was able to leave the horse outside. I paid the hotel manager to get food and water for Herat, and took the guitar into the lobby to see who was there. There were seven or eight people in the lobby. No one I knew.

"Does anyone here know Barry and Dave?" I asked loudly. Three guys came over.

"They're in Peshawar." one said.

"Yeah I know. Are you guys going that way?"

"Yeah. Why?"

This was gonna be a little odd. "I'm traveling by horse. He's outside, and…"

"You have a horse here?" They all ran outside. Herat was eating. Hardly demonic at all. "Nice horse!" "You're traveling on a horse? Where are you going?"

"To Peshawar," I said.

"No you're not," one of them said. "That's in Pakistan. Through the Khyber Pass."

"Yeah, that's the way I'm going."

"You can't go there. Those are bandit lands. You can go through in a car or bus and they'll leave you alone. But you can't go on a horse. Are you going with a caravan?"

"No I'm going alone."

"Alone? Are you bringing a gun?"

Since I had told people I was riding through this territory almost everyone had said the same thing. That I needed a gun to make it through the Khyber Pass. But that seemed completely wrong-headed to me. Guns were their business. I wasn't going to out-gun a Khyber Tribesman. And ….I felt protected by…this is difficult to say…by the fact that I meant them no harm. That I was … all right, and they would know it.

"No, no gun."

"You're crazy," they said.

"Yeah but listen. I need someone to take my guitar to Peshawar and give it to Dave and Barry. I can't take it on the horse."

"What kind of guitar?"

"A Fender acoustic 12 string."

"Can we play it while we have it?"

"Sure."

"I'll take it," said one.

"Yeah, we'll take it," said another.

I looked at them. I had no real choice, and they looked – all right.

"OK then," I said and handed my beautiful Fender 12 string acoustic guitar to three hippies on the road in Kabul.

"Sounds good," the guy said. "We'll get it to Dave and Barry but they'll never let you out of the country on a horse. You'll have to go back and take a bus."

"Whatever happens," I said.

A while later I walked the horse out of the city on the road toward the Khyber Pass.

I knew it would take us days to get there. I had a map that I had found, but it was from Pakistan and except for the river and one town, Jallalabad, there was nothing on the Afghani side of the map until the Pakistani border. After that there was some detail and beyond the pass it was a straight run into Peshawar. Between Kabul and the pass was pretty much uncharted, at least on my map, and I really didn't know what to expect.

Outside the city I mounted up and rode. It was much easier without the guitar. By now the afternoon had became late and the shadows grew long. The land flattened out and I was in the desert. This is not desert like the Sahara with windswept hills of deep sand. The ground was hard and dry and largely barren with an occasional dried up little bush. Very little green. There was nothing much to see except some mountains in the distance. Then way off to my right, a couple miles away, I saw something moving my way. Someone was running across the desert, cutting across at an angle that looked like it could intercept my path. It was a long way and it took a real effort. It began to look like a child. Why was a child working this hard to get to me? It had to be more than simple curiosity. A few minutes more and he was getting close. Definitely a child. What could he want? After ten minutes of running he reached the road behind me and although too far away, he bent down, picked up a rock, and threw it at us. Amazing.

I had figured that I could crash in the outskirts of the city. That there would be a few shops and houses, a chi shop, and someone would accept a little money to let me tie up the horse and crash outside. The problem that quickly developed was that there were no outskirts to Kabul. Once you got out of the city there was nothing. The road. And the mountains in the distance. It wasn't dark yet, but that was coming soon. Time to wrap up this first day on the road. I could turn around maybe and find some place back in the city, but that would take a couple hours, it would be dark and that would be back-tracking, which I never wanted to do.

I rode on. It was twilight now. Just then I saw a light up ahead a mile or so. Maybe this would be a chi shop. I spurred Herat on a little. The horse was sick of this day but he perked up a bit. As we approached I saw that the light was outside a small mud building. There was no sign of anyone. I turned into the path and got off the horse. "Hello!" I called. (The universal hailing signal.) Two guys came out. They were pretty amazed to see me. Could I crash by their house? They indicated I should come inside. First I had to tie up Herat. I had a metal stake I was carrying to tether him when there was no tree. I banged it into the ground out front by a little scrub for Herat to eat and went into the building.

Inside it was filled with milk. Stacks of racks of filled bottles. It was a milk station. Great. I was lucky to have it. The guys seemed real nice. They had me lead Herat around back and one of them tethered him there. I went just out of his reach and rolled out my sleeping bag. I got in and craaaaaasssshhhed. But wake up! It's four am and someone is yelling. It's the milk boss and what the fuck is this guy and his horse doing here? Against all regulations!! And Herat, to top it off has dragged his tethering stake out of the ground and is happily standing in the middle of their little vegetable garden, eating, eating, eating.

Mud house with charpoy bed on the outskirts of
Kabul on the road to the Khyber Pass
(Collection of the author)

Kabul Gorge

So I left the milk station early and abruptly and found myself out on the road.

Today was to be the day certain things would be established. The first had to do with speed. I had assumed that I would ride for a while and walk for a while. It didn't seem fair to ask the horse to carry me all the way. Maybe this is crazy but I felt that this horse, who had spent most of his previous existence (as far as I knew) just going out for a ride or two each day, shouldn't be asked to carry me for 11 hours every day while we traveled. I knew we had to keep moving but I felt that part of that time I should be walking with the horse. I figured that would slow us down some, but I was walking at a brisk speed since I had a long way in front of me. While I was riding I found that I couldn't expect the horse to gallop very far, it wore him down quickly. And then he walked. What I discovered was that when I was walking, I walked at the same speed the horse walked when he carried me. So it made no real difference whether I walked or rode. I just had to keep going. Either way we covered the same distance, which turned out to be about 30 miles a day.

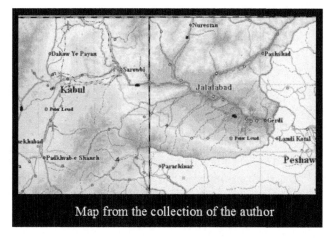

Map from the collection of the author

I started out this second day wearing the cape Dave had given me. It was true that the local horsemen all wore them, and it probably was designed for dealing with the sun, which could sometimes be hot, but it was the beginning of November, and at about 5,700 feet elevation so not really too hot during the day. In addition I have never felt comfortable in loosely fitting clothes. When I make a sudden turn, I like my clothes to make the turn with me. Maybe its because I'd heard that Isadora Duncan had been killed when her scarf got caught on something while riding in an open car. Anyway, I gave it a try and quickly decided that jeans and a T-shirt were the ideal traveling clothes for me. When it got a little cold I put on my jean jacket. Perfect. Just an American thing, I guess.

It was time for my saddle and boots to do their long range stuff. My boots were black pull-on leather boots I had bought used in the market in Kabul. Not quite cowboy boots. Not as heavy as motorcycle boots. Walking miles and miles down a hard dusty road, they stood up pretty well. Nails began to show on the soles and heels but everything hung together. The saddle hurt. Hours and hours on a hard wooden saddle is gonna hurt even when the horse is walking. Readjusting yourself can help only temporarily. I put some of my extra clothes under my ass for a cushion. That kind of worked. It wasn't too bad. No way around it anyway.

The horse felt big under me. Powerful. It still seemed amazing that such a powerful beast would let himself be controlled by me. My power over Herat was not complete. Sometimes the horse fought me to stop to eat something along the road. I couldn't let him think he was in charge but I sometimes let him eat for a minute. I realized that if Herat had his way though, he'd be stopping more than walking. And again he had a strange habit when we were galloping of drifting from right to left across the road until he was running in the rough alongside. As we galloped I had to pull the horses' head to the right to straighten his path. Sometimes even that didn't work and I would have to pull us to a stop before the horse went crashing off the road.

It was still early in the day and I felt like galloping a little. I kicked Herat off and gave him his head. He did like to run. As usual the horse began to drift to the left as he ran. I pulled his head straight but Herat continued drifting off the road. I pulled it further around, with no effect on the horse's route until his head was so far around that Herat clearly could not see where he was running, and we were running full speed toward a three foot high rock off the side of the road.

"There! See where you're running?!!" At the last moment I turned the horse's head straight. (What was I trying to prove?) Herat saw the rock in his path ....and he leaped ...... and we flew over the rock ...... into a big crater behind it .....and out of the hole hardly breaking our stride. Ooooooo.

Another discovery had to do with food. Ramadan had just begun. Out there they called it Ramazan. It's the Muslim holy time when no believer puts any food in his mouth while the sun is in the sky. A big meal in the morning before sunrise and then nothing till after sunset. I had expected to pick up something to eat whenever we passed a chi shop along the route. What I hadn't expected was that when I passed the rare chi shop on the road, they were not preparing or serving food. Since I wasn't traveling after dark, not unless I was near a chi shop as the sun was about to set was there a meal for me. Opportunities for eating were turning out to be slim.

I had been traveling for several hours. The mountains in the distance ahead were starting to look closer. Along the way I had seen pretty much no signs of humanity except the road itself and the trucks and busses that occasionally passed. When they passed me these vehicles often sounded their horns although I was keeping well out of their

way. It seemed that honking as they passed was more of an entertainment for the drivers than anything else, just like the kids throwing
stones. They were trying to scare my horse. They were succeeding.
Each time I saw a truck coming I would shorten up on Herat's reins
with the expectation that they would blare their horns as they passed
and Herat would try to bolt. Sometimes I could keep him quiet,
sometimes it would start him galloping. It became a little nerve
wracking for both of us.

There were very few structures along the way. No houses or
businesses. One closed chi shop. When I stopped there and asked for
food, they waved me away. I kept riding. Sometime after mid-day I
saw something in the distance. It was some kind of large structure
with a bright orange roof. OK, I'd seen Lawrence of Arabia. This
must be a mirage because it looked like .... a Howard Johnson's. I
didn't actually believe it was a Howard Johnson's, but I enjoyed the
fantasy for a while. I'll just stop in for a clam roll and maybe a cup of
soup. As I approached I could see that it wasn't going to fulfill that
particular fantasy but I still couldn't figure out what it was, and what
it was doing in the middle of the Afghan desert. Someone came out
of the compound, a young man in brown camouflage pants, and
waited for us on the road. We drew up.

"Hallo," called the young Afghan soldier. "What is your program?"

"My program?"

"Yes, you are English?"

I figured he meant did I speak English so said, "Yes."

"Good. What is your program?"

"I am riding to Peshawar."

"Ah, Peshawar." He thought about this for a minute. "Have you
any books?"

"No, no books."

"Books are very good for me if you are having books."

"Sorry," I said, "no books. This building is what?" I pointed to
the large structure the man had emerged from. Whatever it was,
maybe there was a cafeteria.

"Military," the soldier said. "Chinese are building."

"This is a Chinese military base?" It seemed unlikely. The Afghans weren't the sort to be happy with foreign military on their soil.

"No," he said. "Not Chinese military. Chinese building for Afghanistan. Afghanistan military."

That seemed more likely. Afghanistan is right next to the Soviet Union and China and many countries wanted to have a presence there for intelligence purposes. Building things for the Afghans was a likely way.

"What is your program?" This was obviously something he had been taught in military English class.

"Can I come in and eat?" I asked. It was worth a try.

"Nooo." That was clearly impossible.

"OK.," I said. "Good bye." I started off. The day was progressing and I had to find somewhere to eat and sleep.

"But what is your program?"

"Bye."

"No books?"

"No books, Good bye."

At one point I saw, off to my right across the desert, a group of people moving in the same direction. They were the Koochis, a nomadic tribe. They lived on the desert and moved back and forth from Afghanistan to Pakistan following what little green there was for their flocks of sheep. They were far more colorful than the other Afghans. Their clothing and their tents were mostly red and black with orange, purple and browns. Their women were not wearing the burka but wore colorfully embroidered dresses. They had some horses and sheep and I thought I saw some goats. Lots of children. But they were always at a distance and I was not to see them up close until the border.

The afternoon was getting late when I reached the beginnings of the mountains. I was following the river now and the road curved around a mountain and I could see it reappearing to curve around the next, then disappearing again. The crude map made no mention of what was in front of me. Later I learned that I had entered the Kabul Gorge, a river canyon, a pathway cut through the mountains by the Kabul River. I found myself winding through the mountains, looking down at the river. Occasionally as I rode the trail had split, one road for caravans, one road for trucks, but here there was only one road cut halfway up into the mountainsides. On my left the steep sides of the mountains rose up in a cliff hundreds of feet high. On my right the edge of the road dropped off precipitously to the rocks and water. Often there was no shoulder at all, just a drop of a hundred feet or so. As much as I could, I hugged the cliff side as I rode, staying as far away from the edge as possible. When trucks and busses came though, I had to move over to the edge because vehicles often would not see me as they came around the bend either in front of me or behind. Many of these vehicles continued to blow their horns as they passed. Now the joke seemed a little too life or death.

Kabul Gorge (Collection of the author)

The afternoon wore on and I wondered if I had made a mistake by entering this terrain so late in the day. Where would we wind up? It didn't look like we'd be getting through this any time soon. I still had no idea of where I was, so I pressed on. I could see the road curving around three mountains in front of me, appearing and disappearing. Whenever I saw or heard a truck I would see it first three mountains distant, then a minute later two mountains distant then a minute after that on the road in front of us. Each time I would prepare by shortening up on Herat's reins and holding him tightly as they went by.

Suddenly three mountains distant I saw something undefinable and frightening. Rushing toward us, then disappearing, I had seen what? It was long and black, with a segmented body. Huge and snakelike rushing down the road in my direction. In the distance I could hear a roaring sound. It had looked like nothing that my mind could sort out. It looked like …. a dragon. Then there it was on the curve of the next mountain down! Closer and bigger I realized that it was some kind of military vehicle, a half track. Half truck and half tank. Clashing metal treads and wheels. Herat had not spotted it yet, but he would, and that would make this moment exactly as danger-ous as an encounter with a dragon. The cliff as usual dropped off a hundred feet to the river on our right. Moving to the left would place us directly in the thing's path. I grabbed the horse's reins as tightly as I could, grabbed the horse's mane as well, and waited the last sec-onds.

YAHHHHHHHRRRR!!! The big dark thing screamed as it ap-peared before us. Herat planted his front feet in a horrified stop, then he was whirling and fleeing back along the edge of the cliff, which was only inches away. On our left. I had to stop him fast and careful-ly before he drifted off the edge, but the horse was running in the *same direction* as the thing, matching its speed, the roar in our ears. To-tally out of his mind with fear, Herat ran along the precipice as I tried to pull him in and I felt myself bouncing forward in the saddle, each bounce taking me nearer to flying off and down the cliff.

I fought the horse to respond, and he began slowing his speed and letting the thing pull away. I drew us to a halt. I was sitting on Herat's neck. I pushed myself back and turned the horse around. There in front of us was a bus that had been following the half-track. It had slowed upon seeing this almost fatal moment and every visible window had a head sticking all the way out, staring at us in wonder. Like in a cartoon. Herat looked up and saw this and began to panic again but I was ready and held him down. The bus slowly passed us and pulled away. And we were alone again, still on the road. Still alive, I was thinking. I hadn't thought much about that till now.

It became dark and we pressed on. There was no other choice, but riding this mountain road in the black of night felt dangerous. Each mountain curve we passed led to another ahead. I got off the horse and walked in front to keep our eyes on the edge. I walked us foreword under the dim starlight.

We continued this way for hours. Then some time later, I began to see a glow in the sky. The farthest mountain seemed a little too bright. It didn't seem to have any light of its own, but some other more distant mountain did. Something was being reflected from mountain to mountain, too many mountains down to distinguish. Whatever it was, we were going there.

As we rounded each next mountain the glow grew stronger until finally we saw it three mountains away, on the right side of the road, overhanging the river, a sudden revelation of light. Then it was gone as we moved forward and when we rounded the second mountain it was a building, big, all lit up, and we came around one more bend, and there, up the road ahead, was a flood-lit building on the side toward the river. It looked like a giant hotel. I knew it wasn't a hotel, but it was a human installation of some sort and I was glad to see it and we were getting in or sleeping in their driveway.

As I approached I saw that there was a gatehouse on the edge of the road. A young man ran out and looked at us with astonishment. He spoke to me. It sounded like German. Without any prompting he led us down a walkway into the giant building. It was a hydroelectric plant. Since it had been built for the Afghanis by the East Germans, all the instructions and instrumentation were in German, and it was manned by German speaking Afghans. No English spoken here, but they gave me dinner and took away Herat to feed him and gave me a bed where I immediately fell into a deep sleep.

The Rider

In the morning I had breakfast with a dozen or so Afghanis. There didn't seem to be any big bosses there, which was probably good for me. One of the workers showed me around the power plant a little, trying to communicate in German, much the same way I used my bad French to try to communicate with Italians. I got the point when I saw the German labels printed above each switch and gauge.

Herat had been fed (they didn't want any baksheesh) and I saddled him up and thanked the workers and walked him out to the gatehouse. Out there was another rider, a local with a cape and a beautiful brown horse all done up in the local fashion, hooded with his bridle decorated with bright colors. I looked at him questioningly and the rider pointed down the road. Apparently I was going to have a traveling companion for a while. I got up onto Herat and we headed off.

The rider started off at a pace that was something like a trot. I tried to keep up but after a few minutes had to let Herat slow to a walk. Then after a few minutes we galloped up the road to catch the rider ahead. The local kept his steady pace. Try as I might I couldn't keep Herat going that speed. As a result we rode together occasionally but more often I was falling behind and catching up. The local didn't seem to mind.

Before too long we emerged from the Gorge (thank you) onto a flat road again. We seemed to have descended to a lower elevation and the air was significantly warmer. Now and then we passed a small house or chi shop but as usual these were of no use as a source of food until we arrived at a little village, Sarobi. In the village was a small market area and I was able to find some hay for Herat and some pomegranates. I was careful not to eat the pomegranates in front of anyone, which I figured might cause offense since it was Ramazan. I stuffed them into my pack.

While I am standing there getting ready to go, a car pulls up. It is the Germans.

"Hey Les!" calls Hans.

"Hans!"

"Sheila," I say as Sheila steps out of the car.

"And here you are," she says.

"Here I am." I smile but Sheila again has her distracted look.

"But you still don't need back your pack," say Franz.

"No," I say turning to Sheila. "Are you headed to Peshawar?"

"Then straight on to Pindi and Delhi. Let me take your picture."

Sheila had me stand in front of Herat and she took a picture of me and my horse. The only one ever taken. Then they got in the car, said goodbye, and sped away. And I was alone again, in a foreign village, in the middle of nowhere.

The rider had disappeared for a while but turned up and we hit the road again. As the day wore on I began to notice something funny about the sound of Herat's hooves. I seemed to detect a difference in the sound of one as it hit the ground, sort of a clop clop clop clink. The only thing I could figure was that one of his shoes was wearing loose. The rider was a horse professional so I stopped him and motioned for him to listen and walked around him in a circle. Clop clop clop clink. I could definitely hear something. The rider looked at me then grabbed my saddle blanket as if to show me that the problem was there. He was obviously not going to be much help with this one. We rode on.

Later in the day the land had not changed much, still flat, still barren. Still pretty much devoid of habitation. Again we passed a closed chi shop. I began to wonder about where we were going to sleep. I hoped that by following the rider I could find somewhere suitable, hopefully a chi shop that was cooking. It was getting close to dark and I intended to follow this guy wherever he went. The land became a little hilly. Since I was still falling behind and catching up I sometimes lost sight of the other rider. Just before dark we were entering a small village area and I was racing to catch up to him after he had disappeared over a hill. When I got there he was gone. I rode slowly past the houses but there was no sign of him and I quickly found myself back out on the empty road. I had been ditched. Thanks buddy.

I rode for a while longer in the dark, but soon realized that there would be no real shelter for the evening so eventually I pulled off the road at a spot near a tree, where there was a little brush for Herat to eat, gave him the hay, and ate a couple delicious pomegranates. Then I rolled out my sleeping bag near the tree, and climbed in. I have this ability to sleep soundly when covers are pulled up over my head. Think of that, how in the midst of that alien clime, I pulled my bag up over my head so I would hear nothing, and went to sleep.

Jalalabad

In 1838 the British, who were comfortably ensconced in India, decided to go up and take over Afghanistan too. First of all the Russians were nosing around up there in Herat, and anyway they assumed that the Afghanis would be happy to see them coming in with modern civilization and would greet them with great affection. There's a familiar sounding blunder, eh?

The Governor General, who the British had left in charge of India was a guy named Lord Aukland. He was considered "wish washy" by his officers and was generally cowed by his two sisters who lived with him. His "aid de camp", his advisor, was a weasel named McNaughton. This was all basically his idea. Nobody knew shit about the Afghan people or their culture or cared.

There was also a guy named Burnes around. He was the young political officer, who hung out with the Afghans and knew what was up better than most. Countries send political officers out to spy and cut deals for the government back home. All very swashbuckling. Also, back then there was less proscription against sexual activity in Afghanistan, and the Afghan women can be quite beautiful. Burnes had more than one Afghan girlfriend during his time in Kabul. Back home in London, newspaper readers followed his adventures like a dime novel. They called him "Bokhara" Burnes because of a previous great adventure.

So the British sent McNaughton and an army of about 15,000 soldiers on a long march up through the south of Afghanistan to Kandahar and then eventually up to Kabul to kick out Dost Mohammed, the current Afghan ruler. Now, an army needs more than just soldiers. It needs many man servants for the officers, and animal handlers, and everybody's families too. And it needs Bazaar girls (prostitutes), and after all, you still need your personal gear (one general required 260 camels to carry his). So this army traveled with about 40,000 camp followers, mostly Indian families, as well as 8000 horses and around 30,000 camels. That's a big bunch and very unwieldy to move, but they eventually crawled into Kabul with their new puppet shah and his 600 wives, and set up shop.

By a year later they had been disabused of any notions about the congeniality of the Afghans toward invading armies. And it was expensive keeping the sizable British force there, so as a cost saving measure the Brits decided to reduce the bribes being given to the fierce local tribesmen to leave them alone. As a result, travel through the Khyber pass became hazardous to impossible. One General who was leading a part of the British Army back toward India got bogged down in fighting with the tribesmen and had to hunker down in the fort at Jalalabad, halfway between Kabul and the Khyber Pass. Then in early November, Bokhara Burns, and a few of his friends were hacked apart in the bazaar, their heads stuck on poles. Oops.

Things quickly went from gruesome to worse as the English lost control of their storehouse of food and supplies, which they had unwisely placed just outside their camp. Now they were stuck in their compound in Kabul with little or no provisions. They contacted the general that had made it to Jalalabad asking for some quick help, but his hands were full, and he figured it would be madness to try to march his already shot up men back through the Khurd-Kabul pass (the Kabul Gorge) in November. The army in Kabul made an occasional foray out to battle the locals who were now in full revolt, but their civilized methods of fighting (march out in red uniformed rows) proved inappropriate against tribal sharpshooting.

Around this time a new Afghan leader appeared. Akbar Khan, was the son of Dost Mohammed and generally had the support of the various tribal chiefs. He suggested that some of the officers meet with him to discuss the possibility of everyone working together. General McNaughten (the weasel himself) figured it was time to straighten things out, so he dressed up in his fanciest officer of the British Empire duds, and went out with his staff to meet with Akbar Khan, where he was also immediately hacked to pieces. Akbar turned to another British officer and said, "You'll seize my country, will you?"

Then Akbar suggested that the best plan would be for the British to withdraw to India with him as an escort. They would just have to leave behind most of their weapons and all their treasury and a hundred or so hostages.

And so on January sixth 1842, 5000 troops, their wives and families over 17,000 all together headed out toward the Khyber Pass and India, "protected" by Akbar Khan. 10 inches of snow fell and the British saw their base at Kabul roar into flames behind them. Akbar and his protection never showed up. They made it 5 miles that day. 1,200 died from the cold and the bullets of the Afghan tribesmen. Akbar sent word to say sorry, but he couldn't control these wild men.

The next day the group entered the Kabul Gorge and things became infinitely worse. As they waded trough the icy waters of the river, a continual onslaught of rifle fire poured down on them from above. Soldiers, women and children, babies, camels and horses, lay dead and dying every step of the way. By nightfall the remnants straggled into a cold makeshift camp. Corpses lay all around. There was no food or shelter.

By the 11th of January the survivors had made it only half way to Jalalabad. 12,000 were dead. Most of the women and children had been killed or captured. Every step of the way the army bravely tried to protect their people from the constant attack of the local tribesmen, but inevitably, one by one they fell to the Afghan bullets and knives. By the 13th of January those left had made it to the hills of Gandamak, thirty miles from Jalalabad. Here the attackers finally swarmed over them and with the exception of some women and children taken for hostage, everyone was murdered. Any who managed to escape that day were tracked down, fought for their lives, and were killed.

Two days later a single rider, Dr. William Brydon, an army surgeon, appeared outside the fort at Jalalabad. Riding a pony, his hands and face slashed, shot three times, he was the only person to make it to the British Garrison. A message to conquering armies.

Let me lead you, naked, hungry, lead you through the laughing city.
— Khyber Fragment

I woke up the next morning to someone nudging my sleeping bag. I looked out and saw Herat's nose. He had pulled out his tether again and was trying to get to a choice piece of dried up greenery that I was sleeping on.

"Hey Boy."

Herat said, "Hhffthhhhrrrrrr." We had a moment.

I got up and put the horse's tether back into the ground without disturbing him. Then I pulled down the last of the hay and grain we were carrying and gave it to him. I took out my knife and cut open my last pomegranate. Do you like pomegranates? You peel off the leathery skin and inside are small masses of juicy kernels. You can take bunches of them into your mouth at once. Each kernel has a seed. You think they're gonna be like grape seeds which you would have to spit out, but pomegranate seeds are smaller and with one crunch the seeds break down and pretty much disappear. And the juice of the pomegranate is as good as it gets. So that was my fine breakfast that day.

My map showed two things this side of the border, the Kabul River, which had run through the Kabul Gorge (which the map hadn't mentioned), and the town of Jalalabad. That was about the halfway point for the ride. I was hoping to stop there for a couple days. I needed some food for the horse and myself, and I wanted to find a blacksmith to check Herat's shoe. I went over to lift the horse's foot. A horse will let you do that if you get into the right spot and lift it the right way. I had been taught that by a girl named Carolyn who had spent a couple nights in the house in Paghman. When I examined the hoof, I saw that the horseshoe looked like it was wearing away.

I was saddling Herat when the rider reappeared.

"Salaam." he said.

"Hey," I responded with muted enthusiasm. I wasn't going to get too romantic about seeing this guy again. The rider waited while I finished and mounted up. Why was he waiting? I guess it's a good idea to have a second rider to travel with. Maybe a little safer. Hard to say for sure. We continued in our usual way together, fall behind, catch up.

Around late morning we crest a hill. The road sweeps down and around in a big curve to the left. At the bottom is a good-sized town.

"Jalalabad?" I ask.

"Jalalabad," he answers.

And then for no real grown-up reason we both yell JALA-LABAD! and gallop off down the big curve, all the way into the town.

When we reached the city we said our so longs (salaams) and the rider was quickly gone. I dismounted and took Herat by the reins and led him through the town, looking for a hotel and a stable and a blacksmith. As I walked the locals looked up to consider us. Many were simply surprised, but more than a few laughed. It was a comment on my folly. Although they had never seen a Westerner doing what I was doing, it was confirmation of the stupidity of Westerners in general, and *this* fool in particular. Why? Why did they think a Westerner on a horse was so foolish? Since I had no real idea about what I was headed into, I had no real idea of what these people saw in my future.

I found a hotel and they directed me to a livery. Next door to the stables was a blacksmith. I was concerned because I was beginning to feel that Herat was favoring one leg. I knew that something like that could cause a real problem for us. I wanted to see that the horse was properly taken care of. I walked him over to the blacksmith. I could see that most of this man's work was mechanical and I wondered if I'd found the right guy. Without a word the blacksmith walked over and lifted Herat's problem foot. He had seen it immediately. He pointed to the shoe and said something in words I didn't know, but understood. "Yes," I said. "Tashakur." "One day," the man indicated with his finger. "Good." I said and nodded. I led Herat back to the stables and told them I would be staying two or three days.

I walked up toward my hotel. It was still afternoon and because of Ramazan there was nothing yet to eat on the streets but as soon as the sun went down I bought some kebabs and nan. I just stood there on the street and ate them. They tasted very very good. I bought more and went back to my hotel.

I slept in the next morning. I listened to the sounds of the city and enjoyed not moving. I had missed the early morning Ramazan meal but I had some nan left over and had found some preserves the previous afternoon. There was a cold pot of tea in my room from the night before. Ummmmmmm. Tasted great

I went over to the stables and Herat was in a stall eating. I went next door to the blacksmith to see how things were progressing. When the blacksmith saw me he led me back over to the stables. He lifted Herat's foot and showed me a brand new shoe. All finished already. I thanked him and paid him and added some baksheesh. I told the man at the stables that I would stay two more days. I wanted Herat to rest and give his hoof an extra day in case it had been hurting him.

Two days following I got up and brought my saddlebags over to the stable. I had been keeping them at the hotel because one side had all my belongings. The other side was for Herat but it was empty. Over at the stables I bought some more grain and some hay. I put the grain in the bag and strapped the hay on top. On the way through town I was able to buy some apples and more pomegranates and some leftover nan, all of which I was careful not to eat till I left the city.

I am just on the outskirts of town when I hear... "Hello!"

I turn to see a guy on a bicycle coming up fast behind us. The guy catches up and circles once around the horse. He is an American.

"What are you doing here on a bike?"

"What are you doing here on a horse?"

"Riding to Peshawar. Where are you going?"

"Nepal."

"Nepal? Where did you start?"

"Moracco."

We look each other up and down and grin.

The bike guy says, "Hey. Do you want to ride together for a while?"

"Sure," I say.

I nudge Herat off and up the road. The bicycle guy starts pedaling. He's fast. I start to trot Herat to keep up, but Bike Guy has to go slow and circle around to stay with us. I push Herat into a run. The bike guy and I keep together but Herat and I are going at our top speed and the bike guy looks like he is just cruising. After a couple of minutes I have to let the horse slow down. Bike Guy circles back.

"You're going pretty fast, man," I say.

"I have a long way to go."

"I can't keep up with you, and I don't want to hold you back. I think you're gonna have to leave me behind."

"I guess so," says Bike Guy. "Well, have a good ride."

"Yeah, (one madman to another) You too. Have a good ride."

He pulls away at an astonishing speed and shortly disappears into the distance ahead. Good luck.

Not much happened for the rest of the day. We continued at our pace and the mountains up ahead began to grow closer. The Hindu Kush. Soon we'd be at the Khyber Pass. Meanwhile, it was just keep moving across the desert.

Just about sunset I had a bit of luck. I came upon a chi shop that was cooking in preparation for the evening meal. For a hundred Afs I was able to get a bed on the porch and a good hot meal, lamb stew and bread. The bed was a common type out there. A charpoy. I rolled my sleeping bag out across woven ropes instead of springs. A little saggy but surprisingly comfortable. Once again I had the opportunity to sleep in the perfect night air.

Pakistani Border

The next morning we started off early, and before late morning was out I found myself at the foothills of the mountains. Soon after we reached the border with Pakistan.

I knew this was going to take some doing. I had always figured that if I couldn't get permission to get through the border crossing I could always take a few hours to ride around it at some isolated spot. Looking up at the mountains I realized that this could be more difficult than I had anticipated. I'd better work out a deal.

The border was a little busy on the Afghan side. There were three or four cars of Westerners and off to the side I could see a large group of Koochis. I rode up to the border building and tied Herat to the post outside. Inside was a table with a couple bored looking Afghans taking passports.

I come in and they notice I am alone.

"How many in your car?" says Afghan Border Guy 1

"I'm not in a car."

"There is a bus?" They hadn't heard one pull up.

"No, I'm on a horse."

"A horse?" They are starting to doubt their language skills.

"Yes, I am traveling on a horse."

At this they stand up and peer out the window. Without another word one goes into a back room and comes out a few seconds later with his smiling superior.

"Hallo!" says the Afghan Border Official. He is happy. Baksheesh is at the door.

"You are traveling on a horse?"

"Yes."

The official goes outside for a look.

"This is a fine horse. A very fine horse. But there is a problem. There is no taking of horses from Afghanistan. It is the law."

"I thought that I might be able to buy some sort of permit from you."

"This will be difficult. I may not be able to arrange this."

"Please try to arrange this for me."

"I will see what I can do. Please come back in a little while."

"OK."

I take Herat over to the chi shop where there is a trough of water. After the horse drinks I tie him up and go inside but, as usual, there is no activity. Ramazan. Not even tea.

★ ★ ★ ★ ★

After an hour or so I go back into the border building. The flunkies get the boss.

The Afghan Border Official says, "It is very difficult to arrange this. It will cost fifteen thousand Afghanis."

That was about a hundred and eighty dollars, which was considerably more than I'd paid for the horse.

"No. I don't have that much money. I can give you two thousand."

That was a little over $20.

"Noooo. (he is horrified) That is impossible. Taking a horse is illegal and this is a very fine horse."

"I understand that you will have to go to very much trouble," I say, "but I am not a rich man and I can not pay anything like that."

"Then you will have to return to Kabul."

"Yes I will return to Kabul because I can not pay such a large sum of money."

I turn to leave. This was not what the official wants. If I go back to Kabul he gets no baksheesh at all.

"Please come back first thing in the morning, and I will try to make other arrangements."

This is all right with me. The border is as good a place to sleep as any and I want to give the guy time to think it through. I also figure that I want to get an early start if I'm going to have to ride around the border crossing.

The next morning I have a predawn breakfast and wait for the official to arrive. I have the idea that the man wants to deal with me early while there are fewer people around. I am pretty sure we will come to an agreement. Getting something is better for the man than nothing. The Koochis are gone, having crossed the border with all their horses.

The official arrives and comes over to talk privately.

"I can let you cross for ten thousand Afghanis."

"I can give you four thousand."

We settle on six thousand, about $65. We go inside and the official marks on my passport "with Wasiri tribal pony." Maybe calling it a pony helps get around the law. In any case, I saddle up my horse and cross over into Pakistan.

Landi Kotal

(But he did not believe them. He was a young American fool – Khyber Fragment)

Having crossed the Afghan side of the border I now had to cross the Pakistani side, but there were no restrictions against bringing a horse into Pakistan, so they just stamped my passport and sent me through.

The road from here on headed upward into the mountains. I was officially in Pakistan at this point but I could see that fine political distinctions meant little on the ground. First of all the people were genetically more akin to the Afghans than the Pakistanis. As I have said before, most of the Afghan people seemed Caucasian and not racially like the Pakistanis who are like the Indians. But more importantly, this area clearly didn't really belong to either country. The tribes ran their own show and the Pakistanis obviously respected their power here, as I was later to see.

The road rose higher and higher as it wended its way toward the pass. I could see that going around this border crossing would have been difficult if not impossible. I was glad the border was behind me.

I saw a town up ahead in the mountains. This was Landi Kotal, which I had been told was a smuggler town. As I rode up into the village I noticed that these people didn't laugh at me as I went through. I was glad of that but there was something in the serious way that they regarded me that made me a little uncomfortable. Long steady gazes. Not exactly predatory, more like the way a predator assesses something first to determine if it is prey.

I noticed immediately that most of the men in the town were carrying rifles. That seemed in character. After all they were smugglers. As a rock singer I carried within myself the feeling of an outlaw status. Just a little outside the culture and the law. In some way that must have been reflected in my demeanor because I had always found a certain congeniality expressed by the other outlaws of my society. Bikers, junkies and bad-ass black men often nodded to me on the streets for no apparent reason. I had grown to take it for granted. Here in this smuggler town I was expecting something similar. That they would recognize that any stranger brazenly strolling through their midst was in a distant way their outlaw kin. As I walked these streets I did not feel that. I was an alien. Possible trouble, possible treasure, not their kin.

I looked for a hotel. I knew the Khyber Pass itself was somewhere close before me and remembering the Kabul Gorge, I wanted to have my rest and a full day to assault whatever I was going to encounter. Finding a hotel proved harder than usual. This was a town that travelers drove through. They didn't stop here. There were some small restaurants, closed as usual, but each time I found what looked like a likely place to stay, they turned me away. Finally I found a place where they pointed back to a lean-to in the rear with a charpoy. I could stay there and keep my horse with me. I tied up Herat and gave him some food and water. I gave some old guy in a neighboring stall some baksheesh to keep an eye on things, then went exploring to see if I could find some food in a market.

The streets were lined with little stalls. Commerce was the purpose of this town and goods were exchanged. In many stalls I saw the usual Afghan trade goods, pots and pans, tools, food, clothing. But in many of the shops in Landi Kotal I saw something that I had not seen before. Guns. Some of these were modern looking with obvious military origins, maybe Russian. Some of these looked much older. Some were ancient. Before me I saw the history of the world in guns laid out for sale. I knew little about guns and didn't know specifically what these were, but some looked like Lugars of the sort Nazis used in the movies, some looked like Saturday Night Specials, and some were revolvers. Some looked like rifles out of the revolutionary war. There was something fascinating about this array and I was drawn to look at them, but was never tempted to buy one and I didn't handle or even touch any.

After sunset I bought some kebabs and found some roll-like breads I had never seen before. I went back to my rope bed and ate and crashed. Tomorrow would be a big day, I assumed. I was a little too right.

Khyber Pass

The Khyber Pass

*They stood with their guns strung listless at their backs, impotent against so frag-
ile a marvel, so revealed a fool. "Here is the dreamer," I thought, "in a dreamish
land." "Here is a stranger," they whispered to the land. A land baked real. A
land devoid of dreams. – Khyber Fragment*

Mountain air. Yes, there is something about it. It's more than fresh.
The mountains in the morning feel like new beginnings. The vegetation was scarce, and the sun was strong. The air felt full of energy.
The morning chill quickly dissipated and as I rode, upward and upward, I felt that this had all been worthwhile. That this was an adventure worth having.

I am riding up a long straight hill when I see something up ahead
that looks like a military roadblock. It's the Pakistani military. I draw
up to them. As usual they are amazed.

"Hello," I say.

"Where are you going?" says the tall young Pakistani officer.

"Peshawar," I say and point ahead.

"You plan to ride this horse through the Khyber Pass?" He is incredulous.

"Yes."

"We do not control the road from here until the other side of the
pass. You cannot go through here. It is not safe."

"There is a law that says I can not go?"

"No, there is no law but we can not guarantee your safety."

By now the entire group has gathered around and is inspecting
me and my horse and pack.

"It is better that you return the way you have come," the officer
says.

"I will be going this way." I point again up the road toward the pass. "I take responsibility for myself."

Shaking his head, he stands back, "All right then." he says. and begins to smirk. "As long as you understand we do not guarantee your safety."

"Yes, yes."

I begin to ride up past them. At that, they all start to laugh. Why? These are sometimes a cruel people. They are laughing at me because they believe I am riding to my death.

The road weaves up over higher and higher ridges. The sun is very bright and less and less grows on the ground. Sand and rocks and sun are all I see as we climb and the road winds upward.

Around midday we crest a hill and I can see from mountain to mountain to mountain. The land around me is almost completely barren except for one small stunted looking tree by the side of the road. Next to the tree is a flat rock. I dismount and go over to examine it. It looks like a tombstone set flat into the ground. The words are worn and indistinct and I would not have been able to read them anyway, but the respect that had brought a people to honor this spot and maybe lay one of their own here, is clear to even my Western eyes.

I go over to Herat and pull down some hay for him to eat. Then I pull out the food I have left, those rolls. What better place to stop for lunch. I begin to eat.

I hear a sound. I look up. There on a knoll above me, perhaps fifteen feet away, are two men. Bandits. I assume they are bandits because each one has a large rifle on his back. I am eating. It is Ramazan.

"Salaam Alechem," I say.

Without saying anything one of them comes down and walks around the horse and considers the bulging saddlebags. He is the taller and younger of the two, handsome, as many in the region are. He seems to be in charge. His sidekick is older and like Mazur has a scarred and twisted Hazara face. The two of them circle me as I carefully do not chew what is in my mouth. Then -

"Markino," says the young bandit.

He is pointing to the tree. I don't recognize this word. I am trying to think fast, to think of related words, but all I can think of is maraschino and I look at the tree and the tree is filled with cherries. Gotta be just a crazy coincidence. ... Outlaw 1 grabs a handful and holds them out to me. What could this mean? It is Ramazan. Is it his plan to have me take the cherries, then to shoot me when I have them in my mouth?

"Ramazan," I say. And he says ...

"Man Ramazan, tu nishte." (Something like that.)

And I understand. For me Ramazan, you not. So I put the cherries into my mouth. They're ripe and sweet. I'm hungry and food has been scarce. The outlaw hands me some more.

"Tashakoor," I say and I start to put them in my pack. Then the two tribesmen smile and begin pulling down large handfuls until there are obviously more than I can carry and ...

.... and then there are suddenly a dozen men. A dozen men in a circle around me, each with a rifle. No smiles on these. These are serious bandits. This is serious. I feel the bottom of things falling away.

"Hello," I try.

They do not answer. I am in the middle of nowhere, protected by nothing. This is the moment I have been warned against, have not believed in, and it is here. Their eyes are cold. Very cold. I feel fear, panic, start to rise inside me, up into my throat. And then, clear as day, I have a vision – that my panic will burst out on to the surface, that they will see it and that, like blood, it will draw them in, causing greater panic, causing them to lean in further until everyone is in a whirlpool that descends to me lying dead on the ground. A death spiral. I see it and I see my end, my death, right here, now. And I force that panic back down into my gullet, my trembling gut, and I fake a smile. I nod and greet them, and although they do not respond, they do not attack.

We stand there and regard each other for a long moment. I decide it's time to go. To try to go. I finish packing my horse and get up on him. On my beautiful horse with bags filled with unknown Western riches. They stand in their silent circle around me. I start to walk my horse through the circle, past the men and the guns. I feel the pressure of their stares behind me. In my back. The expectation of a bullet in my back. Step. Step. I turn in my saddle to look back at them. They have not moved. Their eyes remain locked on me. I wave. They do not wave back. And with that pressure and that expectation unrelieved, I ride on for a few hundred feet, always with the pressure of the bullet, until I turn the curve of the next hill and leave them behind.

I do not know for sure why they did not kill me but here's what I think – These are honorable people. They saw I meant them no harm, so they gave me safe passage.

One year later, two American brothers were walking around the world with a donkey and a wagon, and had arrived at a place very close to this, when they found themselves being approached by a group of armed men. As had been suggested to them, they took out a shotgun and fired it once into the air, and were immediately cut down in a hail of bullets, one seriously wounded, one dead.

Peshawar

The rest of that day passed in a dream. I kept finding myself further down the road as if I had been sleepwalking. Sleepriding. Had I been lucky? Or had I been right all along? Even if all my naïve assessments had been correct, it felt like fate had been tempted and might not prove so merciful in the future. And then I looked up and I was emerging from the mountains where the ancient floodwaters had spilled onto the plain of the Indus Valley.

At this point the vehicle road had split from the riding path, and was some distance off to my right as I rode. Cars and trucks continued to hoot at me in earnest. Even from that distance they wanted to reach me, scare me and the horse if possible. Then, when the road was maybe a hundred feet away, a passenger in a car going by, leveled a rifle out his window at me. Those people up in the pass for all their reputation did not point their guns at me. These people in this civilized area aimed their guns at me for fun.

In the years since, Afghanistan has been in constant turmoil as the planet's super powers have decided that it would be useful and easy to roll over them with all the military technology of a psychotic world. First the Russians and now the Americans have sought to subdue these tribal regions for their own purposes. As I have watched this I have known something that the leaders of the modern world's governments have not – that these people will never lie down, they will never roll over and accept a conquerer no matter how benign we see ourselves. That these invasions are doomed along with many of our young who will die because they are fighting a people who fight for their homes, who have almost nothing except the determination never to be conquered. Wouldn't we hope to do the same?

★★★★★

It took a while to reach the city of Peshawar, but by late afternoon I was riding up a main boulevard. A mile or so later I passed a large field on my left where men were running horses. It looked at first like a polo field but when I got further I saw that it was military. It was the horses of the Pakistani army. As I rode I saw long lines of well tended stables, all white and freshly painted. I turned into the compound, dismounted, and walked up to a gatehouse.

"Hello. I am looking for a place to board my horse for the night."

The guard holds up a finger for me to wait and goes and brings out another soldier who speaks English.

"I am looking for a place to board my horse for the night."

"We do not board private horses here, but perhaps some arrangements can be made."

I listen to the musical song of English words as they are spoken by both the Pakistanis and the Indians. See the tilt of the head.

After some discussions on a telephone the officer directs me toward the stables. These are incredible stables, large and clean with many men working in them.

"This is horse heaven, Boy." Herat agrees. All the horses are giants compared to him. Army horses meant to intimidate crowds. Another officer meets me there.

"You can leave him here overnight. You must take him away tomorrow morning."

"Great. How much will it be for his food and stable?"

"No, no money."

"Thank you very much."

And they lead the horse away.

I knew I wasn't in the main section of town where travelers stayed so I didn't expect to meet up with Dave and Barry right away. I didn't know exactly where they'd be and figured I'd search around the next day. I found a place near the stables. It was still Ramazan here too, so I had to wait a while for dinner.

Next morning I had some breakfast and went over to the army base. I didn't see anyone I recognized so I went to the stable where Harat had been led and looked around for him. He wasn't there.

"I'm looking for my horse." I speak to a Pakistani working there. The man shakes his head at me. I go outside and find a soldier.

"Speak English?"

"Yes."

"I'm looking for my horse, I left him here overnight."

"Oh yes, I'll get someone." He goes over and says something to an officer, who looks my way but just shrugs. I stop another officer.

"Excuse me. I left my horse here yesterday and he is not here now."

"Ah, yes. A white horse."

"That's right."

"I'm sure he will be here shortly."

Be here shortly? Just then I look up at a galloping sound and a huge fat man comes charging up on Herat. The horse is soaked with sweat and wild-eyed. Ill used.

"Hey! What are you doing on my horse?"

The fat man looks at me as if I am a piece of shit, climbs down and gives the reins to a stable boy. He laughs and walks away. I give Herat water, brush him down and get him out of there. I am learning too much about these people too fast.

★ ★ ★ ★ ★

Letter from Milton November 13 1970 at the Peshawar American Express office

Mr Leslie Braunstein
c/o Peshawar Poste Restante Pakistan

Dear Les

I have just received your letter from Kabul and now I pray to the spirits that this letter reaches you. The local Pakistani Bank tells me there is no such address as the one you have given me.

I have cabled $1,444.48 to you leaving approximately $1,800 in your account.

Your travels, especially your latest means of transportation must be quite exciting. If I were able to walk away from my office responsibilities I would be thrilled to take a pony ride with you.

To say "enjoy yourself" would be mere surplusage. So stay well and keep in touch with me.

Best regards, Milton.

It took a while but I found my way over to the part of town where travelers stayed. There was no sign of Barry, Dave or the guitar, but first things first. I had to find a home for Herat. Are you surprised, friends? Did you think I was going to bring him home in my luggage? Or maybe ride the rest of the way around the world at thirty miles a day? No, it was time for me and Old Paint to part ways. Of course I had grown very attached to him, but I knew it had to be done. I had traveled alone with a horse. It will be one of the highlights of my life forever, but it was over. My real concern now was to find him a home with someone other than an asshole like the guy at the stables. I speak to the manager at a large tourist hotel. He has been nice enough to say I could keep Herat on the grounds.

"I wonder if you can help me?" I put down two hundred Afs for baksheesh. "I need to sell this horse, right away. I want to find a good owner. A good man."

"Yes," he says, "I will speak to some friends this afternoon."

Later that day the manager comes and finds me in my room.

"Someone is here to look at your horse. Please come downstairs."

I follow him down to the front yard. The hotel is on the outskirts of town next to some open fields. There is a man waiting out front. He doesn't speak English but he's dressed in Western clothes. He looks like a rich young man. I am still very concerned after yesterday's experience. I won't sell Herat into abuse. At least this guy isn't fat. We nod hello to each other and I motion toward Herat's saddle sitting nearby. The young man shakes his head and doubles Herat's rope through his mouth and leaps onto the horse's bare back. And using the doubled over rope as reins he goes galloping across the field. He makes a long circle and then gallops back. He jumps off the horse before he has come to a complete stop. He examines the horse's feet one by one, and then peers into his mouth, then finally his eyes. He speaks to the horse. The horse stands still as if under the control of a master. This is the right guy. The man speaks to the hotel manager who asks...

"How much?"

"A hundred dollars," I say. "And he gets the saddle."

The manager speaks to the man. The man looks at me, in my eyes, as he had the horse. He nods, "Yes." No bargaining, for the first time in the East. It is a very good price for such a fine horse.

★ ★ ★ ★ ★

The next morning I wake up early. I've bought a can of dry porridge and have cooked it up in a saucepan. I've made a lot more than I can eat because I know there are a lot of travelers here at the hotel and I figure someone will want some. When it's ready I take the saucepan and go into a large dorm room where a dozen or more people are waking in beds and on the floor.

"Anyone want some porridge?" I call out.

"Yeah, I'll have some porridge," says someone jumping up in front of me. It's Dave, and he's laughing in my face.

Travels with Donni

SWAT

What is life without someone to share it
What is home without someone to care if
you're coming home? – Companion

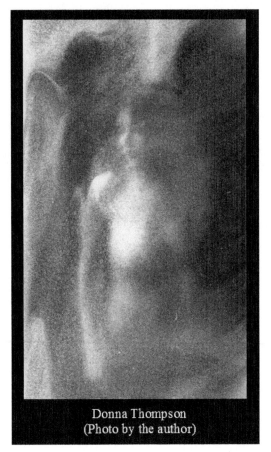

Donna Thompson
(Photo by the author)

Barry and Dave had moved on up into the mountains, to an area called Swat. Yes, they had my guitar, and Dave had come back down to Peshawar to find me.

We got a bus up to Madyan, a village overlooking the Swat Valley, high up in the mountains, deeper into the Hindu Kush.

We stand by the hotel and look down into the valley. Way down. Like looking from a plane, an experience, you'll remember (from the first book that you haven't yet read) that I had not yet had. The valley spread out below us, like the enchanted land in a fairy tale. Green and brown and greener, and cut everywhere with water shining like mercury in the soon to be setting sun. Creeks and pools and the river, like mercury and chrome in the distance below.

Swat is actually the home to many fairy stories. Lots of tales of Djinns. Magical creatures with the ability to disappear and reappear somewhere far away. Djinns. Sounded like genies to me.

Donna (Collection of the author)

So here I am at a town in the sky, land of the genies. and I hear Barry's voice laughing inside so Dave and I go in.

Barry is sitting back, enjoying a smoke and a laugh with some new friends. An English guy and this English girl. Hmmmm. She is laughing at Barry with gusto, and he is enjoying it. Good spirit on this girl. Nice smile. Blonde hair. Sweet face and lovely body.

Barry looks up and speaks from the bed, "So the cowpoke has returned to us. How's your ass, Cowboy?"

"My ass is glad to be here and off the road."

"This is Keith and Donna."

Keith waves and Donna steps forward and takes my hand with a smile. "Hi. Heard you've been having quite an adventure."

There it is again. That instant frazzling of my nerves. A slight chatter in my teeth that tells me I am in the presence of a woman with a power over me.

"Uhh. Yeah," I say and stand there just looking at her.

"Quite a talky one, aren't you?" She laughs at me but I don't mind. I like her laugh. Her eyes that look right at me and stay there.

"Let's check out the sunset," says Dave and heads back out through the door.

"Oh yeah, sunsets are good up here," says Keith and he and Barry and Dave all go outside. Donna and I are left alone.

"So that's your guitar, isn't it?" she says pointing to a corner by Barry's bed.

"Oh yeah." I go over to where my guitar has been stood carefully in a corner. It's the first time I've seen it since it went off on an adventure of it's own. I unzip the case. I have entrusted this instrument, this friend, to some hippie travelers in Afghanistan that I had known for ten minutes. And here it is. It has made its way to Madyan, just as I have. A town neither of us knew when we said goodbye. I slide it from the leather case. I examine it.

"Is it OK?" Donna asks.

"Looks like." I pick at the strings. It is wildly out of tune but clean and cared for. Probably a revered object as it traveled. I tune quickly. Then I strum the guitar. That rich 12 string sound rolls across the room.

"Oooh," says Donna.

I begin playing. It feels good to have my guitar back in my hands. Now as I listen to it, it seems incredible that I risked it this way, but then, that's life on the road. I look up and notice that Donna is watching me closely. Again I feel something in my throat. Wordlessly I let the sound of the guitar reach out to her. She has unbalanced me with her strength and great sexual appeal, but here with my fingers I have a power of my own.

"Is Keith your boyfriend?"

"No. Just traveling together for a while."

"Ah."

I continue playing but now there is only me and this woman. I cast my music over her like a net, to capture her, bring her in, but I am captured too, both lost, bound into something stronger than ourselves.

I stop playing and just stare at her. Her friendly face. The curves of her body, her legs, her thighs. I put the guitar down and walk across the room to her. She stares into my eyes as I approach. And then without logic or preamble we reach out to each other and are kissing hard. I am feeling something like a deep thirst for her. Not just for a woman or sex,...for her. It's like I have been yearning all along for this woman, though a few seconds before I did not know she existed. As I grab her, hold her, kiss her, I know how improbable this is. Without reason or explanation. I only know that I want her madly, and miracle of miracles, she is responding in kind and makes no effort to slow our conflagration. Maybe there was no reason for starting this, but there is certainly no reason for stopping. And a genie might be involved.

This woman is incredibly sexy. That laugh. Her body. Live eyes. And she seems to do exactly what she pleases. That's the sexiest part. Well, there's only one place a moment like this can go. Together we open her shirt. I am staring at her beautiful breasts and then we are both dancing around to get our pants off. From there to the bed in another six seconds and a few more and we are fully engaged. Then, Wooohhh! I am coming like a goat. Pretty much immediately.

Wow. How did that happen? We look at each other and laugh but we are both kind of amazed. In the next year as we travel together, lovers and best friends, we will make love many times in many places, but this was not making love. This was intense fucking that seemed to have been ordered up directly by the protoplasm. "Let's make these monkeys dance," squealed the protoplasm. And we danced.

The travelers sit together making plans.

Donna says, "I think I've had enough of this place."

"Because of the girls?" asks Dave.

Two women travelers had taken a walk up the mountainside to enjoy the day. It was chilly so they were well dressed, provocative only in the sense that they were not veiled or hidden away like the local women. They had stopped for lunch at a spot overlooking the spectacular view when a stone whistled by their heads. They turned to see a young boy, a goatherd of maybe ten years. He was bending over to pick up more stones.

All the children regularly threw stones at the dogs that wandered the hillsides in the day and howled in the night. That was a popular form of entertainment. There was no care for the pain they caused. These were purposeless beasts. Making them yelp and scream was part of the game.

To the boy, these girls were something similar. He had learned from his elders that Western women were immoral infidels. Whores. Not women like his mother or sisters. Not really women at all. And here on the hillside they didn't even have the protection of their men. And what were they doing here anyway? Real women were at home working. He threw another stone. It hit one of the women in the side. She yelled.

Both women had picked up stones to throw back, but he was above them and was much better at this. He threw hard and straight. Like a man. His next stone hit the other woman in the side of her head and she called out in fury and pain. Blood began running down her face. This delighted the boy. He scrambled to get more stones and ran towards them flinging his rocks with accuracy and effect. Soon both women were running down the hill with bloody heads and faces. The boy couldn't leave his goats so he had to stop following. He listened to the sounds of their foreign cries as they ran off. What fun.

"Yes, says Donna, "I'm ready to move on."

Barry asks, "Is everyone going to Goa for Christmas?"

Donna says, "Les and I are going."

"I'm going," says Keith.

It was early December and most young Western travelers anywhere near India, were planning to spend Christmas in Goa, on the west coast of India. It was an annual gathering spot for the traveling young. Getting bigger every year.

"Yeah, we'll be there," says Dave. "Sounds like a good party."

"Booze," say Barry.

"Yes! Booze."

They all like this idea. But I don't understand. "They drink there? Hindi don't drink. They consider it one of the 5 heinous crimes."

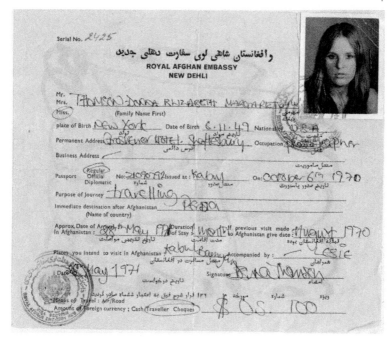

"They're not Hindu," says Dave.

Donna says, "It was a Portuguese colony. Catholic".

"Oh."

"And we Christian's drink," she adds.

"To drink," Barry says and they clink imaginary glasses.

"But the Portuguese are gone," I say.

"But booze is a survivor," Donna says.

"To Booze!" Barry toasts with his joint.

"To Booze!" everyone says.

"So how do we get there? What's the best way?" I ask Barry who seems to know the most.

"Only one way I know of," he says, "overland East to Lahore, then cross the border southeast to New Delhi. And then back west to the coast at Bombay. Then down the coast to Goa.

"Boy, that seems like a long way around. Wouldn't it be easier to go straight to the coast at Karachi, then down to Bombay."

"And how do you get from Karachi to Bombay?"

"Boat?" I am guessing. "There must be freighters. It's right down the coast. Look..its a couple inches on the map."

Donna likes this plan. "A boat would be great."

"No boats," says Dave. "Nothing goes from Pakistan to India or back because of the war."

"What war?" objects Donna. "They're not at war."

"The war they're always on the brink of," says Barry.

Cause there it was. Even these venerable, most ancient civilizations were acting like adolescents. Their newspapers were straight out of the comics. Headlines screamed.. "Fight! Fight the Vicious Monsters!" "Indian Cowards Betray Us Again!" "Our Bombs Are Aimed at Them!" Except these guys were acting like 12 year olds, where Western countries, act more like dangerous sixteen year olds.

"As far as I know," says Barry, "you can only cross the border at Lahore. I've never heard of anyone taking a boat, but who knows? We're leaving in a couple of days on the overland route. If you manage to get there by boat you could get there first."

"Well, we'll see you there," I say.

"Uh huh. "He laughs.

Later Donna sticks her head into their room from the bright sunlight outside.

"Lez. The dateman."

I jump up and go out into the sun. An old man has pulled a wooden cart up in front of the hotel. It is piled high with a huge sticky mound of dates. They are dried and have turned into candy.

"I love these things," I say. "Get a half kilo."

"You know," says Donna, "I could make a damn fine jam out of these."

"Could you? Cause I was thinking.... What if you made jam and I made peanut butter and we sell peanut butter and jelly sandwiches on the beach at Goa for Christmas."

"They'd go nuts for that," she says. "Especially you colonials."

"Yes I imagine that by now most of my poor American brethren would sell their souls for a peanut butter and jelly sandwich."

Picture this.. You are traveling in lands without pizza. Without burgers or fries. Nothing that even looks like a normal sandwich. Remember that meal your Momma used to make? It's not here. And by the way, everything they serve you is spicy hot. Think of the hottest thing you've ever put in your mouth. That's not hot here. Everything from vegetarian to meat to snacks. Most things you eat are hotter than the hottest thing you've ever had. That wears you out. So, want a peanut butter and jelly sandwich as you listened to music on the beach? We were on to something.

"I can make jam out of any fruit they have," Donna says.

"And bread is easy," I say. "There's always bread. Nan."

"Yeah. I haven't seen any peanut butter though."

"No, this is true. But, I think we can make that too."

So we buy some roasted peanuts. They only come in the shell. We open them, then we crush them with a mortar and pestle. Add a little local vegetable oil. A little sugar and a little salt. Pretty close. Close enough for a treat on the beach, but the problem is that it's taking too long to shell the peanuts.

Donna looks at the peanuts we've crushed so far. "A big pile of peanuts in the shell makes a pretty little pile of nuts."

"Yeah, we'll never have enough if we have to open each one by hand. But if we can crush them and then somehow separate the peanuts from the shells... Yeah. Crush up a handful of the nuts in the shell. I'll be right back.

When I return a minute later I have a bowl filled with water.

"Let's see if this works," I say and I throw the pile of crushed nuts and shells into the bowl. The nuts sink and the shells float.

"Lesi, you're a genius," she says, erotically appreciative.

"Our plan is foolproof," I pronounce.

Ah, yes.

Rawal Pindi
and Islamabad

We traveled with our friends through Peshawar to Rawalpindi. Then Dave and Barry and Keith said goodbye and headed east to Lahore.

Islamabad and Rawalpindi are located together. Islamabad is where most of the Muslim religious and government institutions are. That's the nature of a theocracy, religion and government are sleeping together. Just a few years before, the Pakistanis had decided to move their capitol from Karachi to a new spot that wouldn't be so ...well... Karachi. They wanted to start out fresh, so they built a brand new, from scratch, modern city, Islamabad, right next to the old city of Rawalpindi. When Donna and I got there Islamabad had been open for about three years. Still mostly vacant. Pindi was a typical old Pakistani town, roiling with a mostly poor population. People were everywhere and filled every street and public space. Like so many poor populations, they didn't have much to do. No work. No TV or anything like that. You were their entertainment, and wherever you stood or sat or walked, a crowd of Pakistanis, boys and men, followed like a cloud. They are a curious people, these Pakistanis, and that in the end will be their saving grace. Because now they can peer into the whole world electronically, and like all who do, they will see that people everywhere are the same. Humans. Just like them. Even the Indians. Infidels too. Just like them.

And the women, of course, will watch TV and demand their freedom.

★ ★ ★ ★ ★

Islamabad is the center of the Pakistani Muslim religious world. Mosques, schools, administration buildings, new and white under the sun. But religion plays a powerful role in all of Pakistan.

We're in a hotel room in Pindi.

"I'm a bit peckish," says the Lady Donna.

"Peckish?" I don't really know this word. "Hungary?"

"Yes. Let's go find a pudding of some sort."

"Pudding?"

"Dessert, dear. Don't worry, I'll have you speaking English in no time."

"Yes, thank you Memsahib."

An Aussie Guy comes in.

"Hey want to go out for some pudding?" I ask him.

"Oh no. You can't go out there," he says.

"Whaddaya mean?"

"They're rioting out there."

"Rioting?" Donna is concerned. "Why are they rioting?"

"Because some Western guy,' says the Aussie, "a German I think, got caught trying to smuggle hash in a hollowed out Koran."

"A Koran? He cut up a Koran?" She know what this means.

"That's right." We all know what this means.

"What an idiot." I say.

"Yeah. They arrested him and have him at the police station but the people are going nuts. There are crowds running through the streets screaming and waving their fists. Screaming about him. They want him killed right now. Screaming about the rest of us too." Listen.

We all stop and listen, and yes, in the distance we can hear the swell of a great many human voices. Angry. Alarming.

"All foreigners are 'requested' to stay off the streets for their personal safety."

"How long are we stuck inside?" Donna asks him.

"Last time it was two and a half days."

"Last time?" I ask.

"Yeah. They have a riot here every few weeks. Not counting little ones. Some riots I can understand. This one is pretty understandable, but some seem to be just absurd. They don't like what somebody said half a world away, so they're out in the streets threatening death. More for the fun of it."

"Not enough sex," I pronounce.

"Sex?" says my beautiful babe.

"Sexual repression here. More fucking, less rioting."

"Sounds like a political platform," says Donna.

"I do not choose to run. If elected I'll serve myself. Hey, you know what I'm gonna get?" I say.

"What's that, Love?"

"A pudding, made of this nan with some of that honey we bought yesterday.

"Sounds great," she says, "I'll put the tea on."

The riot went on for days. The mob appeared and disappeared at irregular intervals, howling, like any large group of mammals, out of their frustrations, and also their pleasure in flexing muscles they were generally forbidden to use. Their feet running with emotion, their diaphragms baying with the power of their dissatisfactions. To me it felt misguided. Dangerous and indulgent. And repressed. Let's face it. They repress sexuality and their women by covering them in literal shrouds. The Pakistani cities are more Western than other places in the East, so women are occasionally visible, but in Pakistan and in most of the Muslim world the women are still tightly controlled, and for the most part hidden away.

We Americans, on the other hand, celebrate the vision of a woman's sensuality by displaying it to the point of commerce. Although that is not exactly right either, it's a better world for women than places where they will cut off her clitoris so she'll never enjoy sex.

And many of the most religious people out there, including the leaders, seem to have missed the idea that the true purpose of any spirituality would be kindness. Where was their golden rule? Any spiritual path whose leaders are personally mean, is a path that's wandered astray. Stay off it kids. Just say no to unkind religions.

★ ★ ★ ★ ★

We were staying at a decent hotel in Pindi. There was a central room where everyone hung out. There were probably a dozen travelers there of the usual mix: Brits and Americans and Europeans. A couple from Australia. The owner of the place was a very nice Pakistani man who was interested in his guests. He would sit around with us and listen to our stories. He'd never been far from Pindi. One night as a treat we offered him something from a box of goodies someone had received from home. I made him close his eyes and popped it into his mouth. It was a rum cake. Of course, we had forgotten about the Muslim/alcohol thing. The owner jumped up and spit the cake into his hand. He turned and ran out of the room, and didn't come back till several minutes later, after washing out his mouth. I felt terrible and apologized sincerely, and was forgiven.

I used to get zonked out playing my 12 string. The owner and the rest of the staff liked it.

I am playing, and the manager squats across the room to listen. Other Pakis hang out in the corners. The chords that began on the beach in Saints Marie de la Mer have become by now my constant companions. Each time I pick up the guitar my fingers immediately go there. In some way they are telling my story wordlessly, the perfect sound track to everything, and more, they have become a mantra for me and like any mantra are calming, and centering. Gyroscopic.

"You are a master," says the hotel owner.

I snort. "I am not a master."

"Yes."

"Have you heard a guitar before?"

"No. On a recording once only. Not in the room."

"It's this guitar. It sounds really full because it has 12 strings. Two times as many strings as most guitars. A very big sound."

"Yes it is filling the room."

"Outside too," says the owner's nephew, "they are listening also."

"You are a guitar master," the owner says again.

I knew how far from true that was. In fact, I had been playing one chord. An A minor. Over and over. Like a raga. It had played it's way from France to here. A long ever-changing chain of music. Like a sitar might make. Like an Underbelly jam. And the Eastern music around me was now inside me as well, and came out through the guitar. And maybe because what I played was so simple, and because it was infused with my history and that time and place, I had, in fact, mastered what I was playing at that moment. I felt a relief spreading through me at that thought. I felt more relaxed when I played from that moment on. Every musician, especially the self-taught, needs to feel that sometime. That he has mastered something.

There was this guy staying at the hotel – Bad Luck Bobby we called him. Whereas Donna and I were literally having the time of our lives, this guy Bobby wasn't having a good trip at all. He'd been robbed and cheated everywhere he went. Seemed to be having a run of real bad luck. One night some people were talking about a market in town. It was supposed to be very interesting but a little dangerous. Shady. Donna and I wanted to go.

The next morning we find our way over to the market.

"I love this place," says Donna, whirling around to see it all. "There's everything here."

People stop and stare at us. At Donna as she whirls. Merchants call and motion us over. The walls are covered with stalls, mini merchants selling the people everything they want for their lives. Clothes, food, pots and pans, drugs. The same shops over and over. A man sits in his cubical, having tea. He might try to draw you in with words in a language you do not know. "Buy this newspaper you can not read and have passed many times up the block." "Please stop and take a look at these embroidered shirts you have seen everywhere else." Some are unmoving, resigned to the fact that no Westerner will buy from them. Some don't care.

"Hallo." calls a vendor.

"Hello," responds Donna, ever polite.

He is encouraged. "Hallo. Hallo. Yes. Hallo."

"I see where this is going," she says.

"Yes. Hallo! Hallo!" he says.

"Hey look at this." I have picked up a beautiful woven cloth. It's both heavy and silky. Patterned in a geometric black and white. I don't need it, but .... The merchant is trying to tell me something. I'm trying to understand.

"Spread it out... On a table? It's a table cloth. OK. How much?

The merchant says an amount.

"Eighty rupee?" I calculate. Pakistan is an easy one – close to ten rupee to the dollar. That's almost eight dollars. Too much. I toss the cloth on the table and begin to walk away.

"Sahib! Sahib!

I turn and regard him like Bogart would (I imagine). The merchant comes down to fifty rupee- $5.

"Twenty rupee is right. Two dollars." I hold up the appropriate amount. "No," the merchant pleads." That is too low. Unfair. Thirty rupee is fair." I begin to walk away. "Ok Ok, 20 rupee." Sourly, he folds the beautiful cloth for me. I slowly count out some money and give it to the merchant, who looks at it.

"Tashakoor," he says.

I nod and we walk away.

"You gave him thirty rupee, 3 dollars, you know," says Donna

"Seemed fair," I say.

"I'll be doing the bargaining from now on," she says.

"That's probably best."

"Oh look at these!" Donna is standing in front of a stall that's displaying vintage clothing left behind by the British Raj. The British called their time in the Indian subcontinent a Raj. Probably because they lived like Maharajas.

"Oooo, Look as this one Lesi" She gestures to the merchant who points to one wrong thing, then another, until finally the one she is asking about. He brings it down.

"How does this look?"

She holds a brown velvet gown in front of her and pulls it to her throat. She beams at me.

Something slips inside of me. Every day she means more to me, and often because of a moment like this.

"Yes. Let's buy it," I croak.

As Donna haggles with the merchant the crowd gathers, not just the curious and the idle now, but also wealthy young men who are instantly captured by her. They watch her as she negotiates. She is so .. there.

Everyone in Pakistan loved Donna. She was a Western girl, so of course she was a whore, but she was vivacious, very attractive, having blonde hair and LOVELY BOOBS. As we strolled through the market we got chatted up continually, invited everywhere and that day began our career as street royalty. Everyone wanted us. The young rich Pakistanis had money, clubs and parties. What they didn't have was a way out. They were stuck half a globe away from the real action and they were very conscious of it.

Having Donna and me over was a big score for a party. And dangerous. Almost immoral just to have us in the house. These rich kids had booze too. And Donna and I couldn't keep our hands off each other and that overt sexuality made a party really jump. I must confess that during one party for some reason, a game of some sort, Donna and I found ourselves lying in the dark behind a living room couch and .....

Anyway, we made lots of friends that day at the market and had a great time, and when we got home we told everybody about it. "That sounds great!" said Bad Luck Bobby. So he went down to the market the next day, got cheated and got the shit kicked out of him. Hmmm.

★ ★ ★ ★ ★

"Lesi," says Donna one day, "lets go to a hamim. Have a nice hot bath."

"Sounds good. There's supposed to be one a few blocks away. Do they allow women?"

"I don't know," she says, but let's see what we can do."

We go down to the hamim, the baths. It's a large white building. We go inside and step down into a tiled room.

"Hello," I say to a clerk sitting at a table.

"Yes?" He is responding to me but staring at Donna.

"We would like a bath," I say. "You have a hot bath?"

"We have only showers."

"Hot?"

"Yes. Very good, Hot."

"How much?"

"Five rupee."

"I will pay ten rupee for twice as long. OK?"

"Yes. Two times. Yes."

"And the memsahib?" I say pointing to Donna, "You have showers for her?"

"Oh. No."

"You have no shower she could use? Are they private?"

"Yes. If you want."

"OK. Here is twenty rupee. Ten for me, ten for memsahib. Both two times long. OK?"

"Yes."

He leads us toward the showers. No one else is there. The showers are in a row, each surrounded by three six foot tiled walls and a curtain. I go into one and Donna goes into the adjoining stall and closes the curtain. I strip down and turn on the shower. Oh man. That feels so good. The hot water runs across my head and down my body. This is real luxury. Then almost immediately the water runs cold.

"Hey! I paid for two times hot water! "

The hot water comes back on but only briefly. I begin to towel off.

"Pretty short huh?"

"Yeah," says Donna.

I look up and see that a Pakistani man has climbed up and is peering over the wall at Donna's naked body. Not a kid, a grown man. Because after all, she's a whore isn't she?

I take my wet towel and smack it over the wall near the man's head. He squawks and runs off.

"Where'd you learn that?" she asks.

"High school locker room."

Another afternoon Donna went for a walk and found an English church. She was sitting in it enjoying the cool and being away from the hustle and bustle and Muslim men grabbing at her, when the old English vicar came over to talk. He invited her into his house for dinner. She went, I was off doing something, and as they were eating the first course, he asked her if she would mind taking her top off. He assured her that he had sent the staff away, and that he would not touch her. Well, he's a vicar, she thought, so she pulled off her t-shirt and sat topless for the whole meal, quite a fine meal she said, he sat opposite and they made polite conversation. Later, he shook her hand as she left and he said, "Thank you very much."

I had heard that there was an opium den not too far away. I wanted to check it out. I found a French guy who had been there and would take me.

"You're not going this time, Baby," I told Donna.

"All right," she said, "but do be careful please." And off we went to the opium den.

We walked up the steps of a two story building several blocks away. On the way in, the French guy gave me some advice. "They will show you what to do. The important thing to remember is – don't be the last Westerner out. If you see the last other Western guy is leaving you must get up and leave also."

"OK."

We take off our shoes and are led into a room where a half dozen men sit or recline on rugs. A boy of ten or twelve leads each of us to a spot where we sit and are served tea. An old bearded man progresses slowly around the room, stopping for a while at each person. Assisted by the boy he goes through a process that ends with the customer smoking a pipe.

The old man comes over to me. He motions that I should lay down. I have been watching the others. I lay on my side and the boy slides a brick under my head. Yes, a brick is my pillow and it is not uncomfortable. The old man lays down a pipe. It's a long piece of hollow bamboo that leads to a red clay sphere with a small hole on top. He takes out a small glass bottle which he opens. The boy lights a flame. The old man sticks a little metal rod into the bottle. It comes out with a coating of a black tar. He holds the stick over the flame and the tar begins to bubble. He rolls this back and forth across the back of his hand and it forms a ball. Then he puts the stick back into the vial and repeats the process till the ball of tar has grown considerably. Then he quickly jams the stick into the little hole at the top of the pipe and wipes the hot opium out all along the edges of the little hole.

As I lay on my side the boy holds the pipe in my mouth. The old man shows me that he wants this done in one long inhalation. Some of the other Westerners can't get it right, but it's not a problem for a singer with good breath control. I pull as the old man uses the flame to burn all the tar off the edges of the hole. All around and around... Then he does it all again. Then again, and I have smoked three pipes.

The old man and the boy move off but I am hardly there myself. I float in a dream. A very good dream. Warm. Comfortable. Ummmmm. And then the dream becomes strange. Then stranger. I become concerned. Then anxious. I wake up. I shake my head. That was a little weird. Anyway I feel good. Fine. My body feels warm and fine. The brick feels perfect. I drift off into another dream. Different, but again a lovely warm dream. Everything is good. Then something changes and I become anxious and wake up. This reoccurs over and over. This is opium for me. Comfortable, dreamy, to anxious, to awake. Still, it seems like a nice way to spend an afternoon. The old man circles around to me three times. Then the French guy gets up to leave, and I leave too.

I returned the next day and the next. I knew I was flirting with a kind of danger, but I felt I could keep control. Over the next two days I got to know some of the men who were also there every day. I met a man who had been a banker. He had lost his wife, his family and his career because he had taken to spending his days here. The man was so sorry it was true but he was powerless to change. He acknowledged that, and had another cup of tea and another pipe. There was power in this shit. These guys had lost control a long time ago. For three days I dreamed away until the last Westerner got up. Then I got up too, and walked home.

After three days the smell of the opium began to make me sick and I stopped going. Opium was nice but it was not for me. Although I was gonna miss the positive effects on my bowels. For three days, yes three blissful days, I didn't have the famous shits.

The hotel had bathrooms in the hall and a shower on the roof. The building was 3 stories tall. You would climb up to the roof and there was a little room perched on the top which was a cistern and a stall shower. (Cold.) Three stories was pretty tall for Pindi so when you were up there for a shower you got a chance to get a really good view of the city. A great place to smoke a joint.

I was out making arrangements for our train to Karachi. I was walking back to the hotel and was about two blocks away when I noticed that every person on the street had stopped whatever they were doing and were all looking in the same direction. I looked where they were looking. At our hotel. And there, up on the roof, on top of the shower, was Donna! She was standing, lit by the days last sunlight, dressed in a jacket and jeans, feet planted wide, her hands on her hips, scanning the far city, oblivious to the fact that she had stunned the city just below. Later she was to say that it all looked magical, with the sun setting and the smoke from the cooking fires in the dusk, and the call to prayers. But it was she that was magical. On top of their world. Like the Statue of Sexual Liberty.

And to me she was an angel, the epitome of what that sad repression could not control. Willful, wonderful, and I better get her down before more riots ensue. What a girl!

Train to Karachi

At the train station we pick up tickets at the first class window. Everything for us is half price so we go first class. "This is hard to believe," I say looking at the tickets.

"Let me see," says Donna. "No. Look. It says first class...and Its got a number. 8601B." We walk along looking at the numbers on the cars.

"Here it is," she says. "Hey look at this."

"This can't be right," I say. "We get this whole compartment to ourselves?"

"That's what the man said."

"Eleven dollars each for a 24 hour ride all by ourselves in a first class compartment."

"And Lesi look, there's a lock on the door. Uh oh." We slam the door and are immediately on each other.

"Wait, wait, Lesi."

"What?"

"Wait till after the conductor comes."

"Yeah – the conductor. What?"

"The conductor is gonna come by for our tickets, Then we can lock the door."

"Uhhh. Yeah. OK. Right."

There's a rap at the door. "Tickets. Tickets please." We open the door and the conductor enters.

"Here you are," I say and hand the conductor the tickets.

"Two passengers to Karachi. Correct?"

"Yes," I say and "Uh...Will you be coming by again? Or someone else, to sell food or something?"

"Oh no sir. There are no services of that sort. You will buy some snacks, fruits and drinks and such, out your window.

125

"Out the window? "says Donna.

"Yes memsahib. In the towns. On the train we have no such services. Just the toilet at the end of the car.

He leaves and we look at each other. Donna leans to the door and turns the lock with a snap. I cross to her and she pulls me into her arms.

★★★★★

Later -We are both naked. She is lying face down on the berth watching the world pass outside our window. I lie behind her, using her bottom as a pillow which I occasionally snuggle and kiss. I don't know if I can remember a better moment in my life, naked with a beautiful woman watching the exotic world roll by.

"I'm an angel," I say.

"You're an angel? I don't think so." She wiggles her butt.

"Oh yeah. This is bad boy heaven so I must be an angel."

"No Darling," she says, "this is bad girl heaven and you just work here. She turns over and claps her hands for service. I slide up onto her.

"I'm hot and slippery," she says.

"My two favorite flavors. I always order that."

"You don't always want to order the same thing," she says. "Sooner or later you're gonna want a bit of something else."

"And you? Are you on a strict Lesi diet?"

"I don't know. I might like a little nibble of something now and then."

"Cleanse the pallet?"

"Yeah. But you know," she says, "just now I get to fuck my closest and dearest friend, and I'm all full up with that."

I am a little speechless. "Ah sweetie." We kiss and kiss.

Been lots of places
I never planned to be
and Karachi's something but it's got nothing for me
Its got no flowers, got no smile
got no powers and it's got no style
but I'm stuck in Karachi
god I'd give a lot to be

anywhere just not to be
here
not here
not here – Stuck in Karachi

Karachi – Seedy Hotel

"Whaddaya think?" I ask Donna as we step into a bare room with two beds and two windows.

"Looks like all the rest," she says.

"Yeah but two dollars? I thought I'd be takin you to at least a five dollar hotel. Maybe six."

"Well," she says, "we can always leave if its too bad."

We open the door to the toilet down the hall. It is the same hole in the floor with a little water faucet on the wall.

"Same fine facilities," I say. "OK, we'll take the room. We'll need two towels. OK?"

"OK. Yes, yes. OK. Two towels. OK," says the young man whom we are never to see again that day. We enter the room and throw our packs on the beds.

"You want that one?" I ask her. "It's too hot to sleep together all night."

"Agreed. Bring out one of those mosquito coils." I dig one out of my pack and read it. "Lion Brand Mosquito Destroyer!"

"I hope so," she says.

"Well," Doctor Les says, "it actually won't destroy them. They don't like the smoke so they don't try to come in. But any that are already in here are gonna figure, what the hell, and bite us any way. So we're eventually going to have to kill the ones in the room."

Donna grunts. We prepare for bed.

Later-

Light snaps on. I jump out of bed. I stand by the head of the bed for a few seconds then smack the wall with my open palm.

"Die! Look, blood. Our blood."

"Good boy," says Donna. "There's one over here. Could you get it?"

I wait at the head of her bed, then smack the wall over her.

"More blood. Very satisfying. Donna! I'm bloodthirsty! A blood-thirsty killing machine."

"And my hero. Maybe you can squeeze in here for a while."

"You mean like the spoils of war?"

"Like a princess you've just saved. And the only thing I have to reward you with is my virtue."

"You're a virgin?"

"No, and that's my virtue."

I snap off the light.

★ ★ ★ ★ ★

At the steamship office the agent is saying, "Bombay? No. There is no travel between Karachi and Bombay."

"But it's right down the coast," I say.

"Yes," he says, "but it is India. And the situation with India is very bad. Very very bad."

"Yes I know. I see that today's headline is in red." I hold up a newspaper that says in red letters – WE WILL BOMB THE FOUL ENEMY. "But there must be something. A freighter maybe."

"Yes, there is one such ship. Greek. It stops at both ports. But that comes only once every six weeks. The next will come in about one month."

"We wanted to get to Goa by Christmas," says Donna.

"Ah Goa. You must then take a train up to Lahore and from there across the border to Delhi and then another train down to Bombay. Then you may proceed down the coast from Bombay to Goa.

I look at Donna. "That's not happening."

"Nope," she says, "we'll figure something out. Always do."

"Always do," I reply, and it's true. "Hey let's go have lunch at the Intercontinental."

"Sounds Fab," she says.

★ ★ ★ ★ ★

The traveler had a lot of money even if he didn't think so. Everything being relative, you had access (or your family back home did) to thousands of dollars in countries where a thousand is like a million. Everyone wanted your money, that was true, but they could do without you. You had more money than you deserved. Too much money. Local prices were almost nothing to a Westerner. A meal was 20 cents. A hotel could be $5.

Up at the big hotels, where the Western businessmen stayed, a meal was at least two dollars. Could go up to ten. And they ate whatever they pleased (not pig meat). All the time. As much as they wanted. And they drank booze. Forbidden. Well, forbidden to the locals. These infidels had no such rules for themselves. They drank at the big hotels and the richest locals drank with them. And on top of all that, they traveled with whores. Exposed women. Revealed. They showed their faces. Their smiles. So degrading it took a man's breath away. They would be fucking these rich travelers that very night. You had to give it to them, those fucking infidels.

These hippie infidels (and their own whores) were traveling in a different world. It was local and lots cheaper. They had less money, so naturally they got less respect than the bastards at the Inter-Continental hotel. And yet people on the street usually had a respect for even these Americans, because, in addition to having money to burn, we were the model of a people who had prevailed by leading ourselves. America. Almost everybody admired America. Let's be more specific – They loved the idea of America. Generally they hated the self-absorbed American government. But still they had to admire the American people. We were the ones who had said, "Fuck the king". We had ditched the king and the official nobility. We said to them "You have ruled us, and taken all the wealth. Now we will rule ourselves while you take all the wealth. It was good as far as it went. We called ourselves the land of opportunity and it was astonishingly true. Yes, anything can happen in America. That made us the envy of the world. Hope springs here eternally. And that optimism when tested, had gotten strong and won wars. Not to conquer the world.... To set it free. This we had been taught.

Donna and I are sitting at the counter in the restaurant at the Intercontinental Hotel and we are each eating a big bowl of spaghetti.

"See," I say, "the spaghetti is $2 a bowl but they give you another bowl completely filled with grated cheese. Just dump the whole thing in. Very rich and filling."

"Delicious."

A Pakistani man dressed in fine Western clothes approaches us.

"Excuse me. I hope you don't mind my question, but are you Americans?"

"And English," Donna says.

"Yes, I see. If you don't mind my asking, have you just arrived?"

"Recently."

"Well then you possibly do not know about the Christmas Ball. A very big affair. And you would be very welcome. Everyone who is celebrating Christmas in Karachi, will be there."

"Where is it?"

"The Metropole Hotel, on Christmas Eve. Yes, you must come."

I say, "We expect to be gone before then, but if we aren't, we'll keep it in mind."

"Very good. I will hope to see you there." He leaves.

Donna says, "Well that was nice. Nice of him to invite us."

"Let's see," I say, "never saw us before, and crosses the room to invite us to a fancy party. Do you think it has anything to do with your blonde hair and beautiful tits?"

"And my amazing ass."

"And your dazzling smile."

"Do you mind?"

"What? That I get invited places because the men are lusting after you? Not a bit. A woman of great attraction does a man honor just to be with him. Let's blow off the idea about making it to Goa for Christmas and stick around here for the grand ball, where you will be queen."

"And you the prince at my side."

I bow.

"Here Prince." She giggles.

Hotel Room -

Donna is wrapping herself in the black and white cloth as if it were a sari. "This is so beautiful. I can't believe it's a tablecloth."

"You can wear it if you like. You can have it. I don't know why I bought it. Must be for you."

"I love it. You can wear it so many ways. I'll bet I can wear it a different way every day we're in Karachi. Does it look good?"

"Elegant."

"Maybe I should wear this to the ball."

"A table cloth?"

"You said I look elegant."

"And you do. I see no reason why you shouldn't wear a table-cloth to the Christmas ball. It looks like a lovely gown."

"No, I'm going to wear that beautiful brown velvet dress we bought at the market in Pindi. What are you going to wear?"

"I've been thinking about that. I've been thinking that I'd like to have a suit made."

"You? A suit? What kind of suit?"

"A three piece white suit like Sidney Greenstreet and Peter Lorrie used to wear in old movies."

"In the Casbah. I know what you mean. You could do that. They have good tailors here and they're cheap too."

"I was thinking...," I continue, "jeans are made of denim which is like canvas. So why not get it all made out of white canvas and then I can just hose it down like an awning when it gets dirty.

"Sounds very practical," says Donna.

We are in a tailor's shop and the tailor is measuring my leg.

I am saying, "Cut the pants just like these jeans. Double breasted jacket and vest, the same way you always make them. OK? And you make it all out of white canvas. OK? All white canvas?"

The tailor is shaking his head. "Canvas? I am not having canvas. Canvas you are finding only in the automotive section of Karachi. You must buy there and bring to me."

"Write down where we should go. I will buy and bring to you."

"Five yards will be necessary. Canvas tomorrow, suit Friday."

★ ★ ★ ★ ★

It's Friday and we are back in our hotel room. My new jacket, vest and pants are all standing up of their own accord. They look like marble sculptures.

"They look great." Donna says stifling a laugh. "They really do."

"I think," I say, "once they start to bend at the elbows and knees they'll be fine."

"Smashing," she says and laughs.

Loud Pakistani radio is suddenly heard. Turned up to an unintelligible level.

"What's that?" she asks.

"Its that guy down the hall."

"The business guy?"

"Yeah." I say, "he's real drunk and real nasty. He's prowling the halls.

"He's big too," she says. "You've gotta get him to turn it down."

"Great."

"Oh Lesi. You'll do it."

I go out into hall and up to the drunk's room where the radio is screaming. I lean in.

"Hi."

The man looks up, startled.

"Whathe fuck you want?"

"Your radio. Maybe you could turn it down a little...."

"GET THE FUCK OUTTA HERE!!!!!" The drunk lunges toward the door, bouncing back off the door jamb, and landing on his back on the floor. I beat it down the hall.

"Got that all resolved now, have you?" says Donna.

"I'm working on it."

I flip on the room light overhead. As it goes on the poor wiring causes screeching static on the radio down the hall.

"Wait a minute." I flip the switch back and forth and as our light flickers, the radio screeches with static. I close our door and begin flipping our light up and down. After a while the radio is suddenly turned down.

"Well done, you!" says Donna.

"Thanks," I say. "Spoils of war?"

"Righto," she says and makes room on her bed.

★ ★ ★ ★ ★

We have arrived at the Metropole for the Christmas Ball. Donna and I are standing in a circle of admirers. In addition to her gown Donna has her hair twisted up on her head and is wearing serious makeup. She is beyond gorgeous. I am in my suit which actually looks good.

"You are staying long in Karachi?" a local businessman asks.

"We haven't decided yet."

"Well you must stay some while. There are many parties here and the like. You will enjoy yourself very much."

A young officer appears. "Good evening." He bows to me and Donna. "I am Lieutenant Rachid. I am training to be a pilot in the Pakistani Air Force. May I get you a punch?"

"Pakistani Air Force," says Donna, "I didn't know there was one. Do you fly a jet?"

"Well, I am training to fly a jet but I have not yet been in one. We are in a very dangerous situation with India. Very desperate. I think shortly they will begin attacking us and we must be ready to respond with deadly force. We have six jets that we have received from America (he nods to me) but so far we are training in the classroom."

"Sounds like you'll save a bit on jet fuel," Donna points out.

"And planes and officers," I add.

"Fuel is very cheap here. Only planes are expensive. May I get you a punch or some other drink?"

"There is alcohol in it?" I ask.

"Oh yes. Here at the hotel things are much like in your country."

"Punch sounds good," says Donna.

He hurries off. A statuesque Western woman appears.

"Where did you two come from?" she says.

"Hey. You're British," Donna says, "I'm Donna. This is Les from New York."

"Trish. Nice to meet you. Come out here for some D&R?"

"D&R?"

"Drugs and recreation. Don't you know? You can get pretty much anything out here. Heroin, codeine, cocaine, morphine, speed. Everything. And all at pharmaceutical quality and cheap cheap prices. I'll show you around."

"And the police?" says Donna.

"All legal, Darling."

"And that's why you came out?"

"That's why I stayed. I came out for a modeling job. They flew me out to India. Did a shoot at the Taj Mahal. Pretty nasty up close, with the beggars and people pissing wherever they want. I met a Paki guy and he invited me out here. Big businessman. Mr. Hakeem. He's around here somewhere. He'd like you. (looking Donna over) You could do very well out here. You could get $200 a night easy.

"$200? For what?" asks Donna

"She's so cute. For fucking, of course."

Donna has no response to this but turns a bit red.

The officer arrives with the drinks. He sees Trish, hands over our drinks, stammers... "Yes. Your punch."

"Thanks, Lieutenant," I say.

The officer looks up at Trish, drops his eyes to the floor and scuttles away.

"Yeah," Trish says. "Write down your hotel room. I'll come by with a box of goodies. You around tomorrow?"

Donna is still flustered. "Uh, Yeah."

"Sure Trish," I say. "Come by around noon. We'll be there."

"Good," she says. "See you tomorrow. You'll have a good time in Karachi......for a while." She walks off. We stare after her.

In the hotel room I am lying on my bed, reading. Donna is cleaning her new camera lens. She is a very good photographer. She had been traveling with a decent camera but a western junkie had offered to sell me his very fine new one for a junkie price and I had bought it and given it to her. She gave hers to me. And I had bought her a new back-pack from someone else. A real fine one that she coveted. And I had the tailor take the metal brace out of her old one and had it sewn into one of Herat's saddlebags to make a pack for myself.

"Lez. (She always pronounces it Lez.)

"Yeah."

"What do you think about that Mr. Hakeem thing?"

"What?"

"Him paying her $200 to ...fuck him."

"I don't know. It's her business, I guess."

"I've never had sex for money," she says, "but what's the big deal? I like sex, usually. I mean what do you think?"

"I think it would be your business."

"Come on."

"OK, I say. "What do I really think? You're not hurting anybody so its not a moral issue. It's up to you. A woman like you deserves to have good and great sexual encounters in her lifetime. Good and great lovers. It's your right. As for prostitution itself... If someone forces a woman to have sex, that's wrong and terrible. If she's forced into it by circumstance, to feed her children say, that's terrible too. But if she chooses to exchange one of her finest assets, her ability to thrill a lover, for good food, things she likes, and money too, that's her call.

"I know that. Its not the money. Its......"

"Being bought. You want to be bought. Its like a short term bondage."

"No Silly. Being appreciated. Being valued. Something like that."

"Top dollar too."

"But Lesi, that's what you think. What would you *feel* about it? Would you be pissed, or not want me after?"

"Not pissed. I don't know exactly how I'd feel, but it wouldn't be jealousy. I mean, I'd hate it if you suddenly left me for someone else. But we're not talking about that. And I doubt very much that I'd want to fuck you less. As a matter of fact its making me want to fuck you right now just talking about it.

"I've always wondered what it would be like," she says. Maybe every girl wants to try it once. I mean, to have a guy want to give you money, lots of money, because you turn him on."

There's a knock at the door. I get up and answer it. Its Lieutenant Rachid and a younger officer.

"Pardon me," Rachid says, "I hope you'll remember me from last night's Christmas Ball. Lieutenant Rachid. This is my friend Omar. We were hoping that we could stop by. We have brought some local pastries."

Men were always coming by. It was Donna. They all had convoluted fantasies that this western woman would somehow wind up fucking them. A ship's officer had been coming around telling us about tickets he could get for possible ships we could catch to Bombay although in the end we realized there had never been any ships.

But just to get into our room and sip tea with Donna and me who I guess they figured was her pimp.

"Sure," Donna says. "I'll put on some tea."

"Come on in, boys," I say. "Have a seat. So you both learning to fly?"

"Only I. Omar is an engineer. But I am training always."

"Without a plane."

"Yes we have some exercises that we do. For instance. See this fly over the table? We get it in our sites like this." He hold his hands up to his face like a gun site and begins to move around the room following the fly. "We keep it always in our sites like this and..."

At that Rachid bumps into the table, knocking over a bottle and breaking a glass. In the confusion he has dropped his hands and lost the fly.

"Sorry. Sorry."

"OK. Good luck to everybody," I say.

There's another knock on the door. Donna opens it and Trish comes in.

"Hi Trish," I say.

"Hi Les, Donna." She turns to look at Rachid. "Lieutenant..."

"Yes, well, we must be going. Nice to see you again." He nods nervously to Trish, then they exit stage left.

"What was that all about?" I ask her.

"I make him nervous. I know their boss."

"Their boss in the air force?"

"Boss of the air force. So," looking around, "this is pretty basic."

"Works for us," I say.

"Yeah," she says. "So here's what I've got." She opens her case. "These are little morphine tabs. Straight out of the drug company labs. Very clean. You can take about eight of them and scotch tape them into a regular envelope and they'll go right through the post to London or New York. This stuff here is like cocaine but its the pharmaceutical version. Great rush. I've got a little opium, not much, a lump of nice hash, and a couple good kinds of speed.

"How do you take the pharmaceutical cocaine?" I asked.

"Well I shoot it. But you can snort it if you don't like needles."

"We're simple people," I say. "Some hash. A little opium."

"Here's some black Pakistani hash that comes directly from the dispensary."

"The government sells it?" This is a new twist to me.

"Yeah," she says.

"Why?"

"Now, why would I care about that? Want some?"

"Yeah. I'll take that piece."

"And I've got this little ball of opium. Maybe three or four hits."

"That's the way I like it," I said. "I roll it into tiny balls and pop em when I'm tired of the shits."

"Yeah it works for that. That'll be fourteen dollars. I know its high but that includes the carrying costs."

"Fine with me," I say. She gives me a big piece of hash and a little ball of opium.

"So Trish," Donna starts, "Is it working out for you out here?"

"Is what working out?'

"You know. With the men here."

"You mean fucking these guys for money? Its no big deal. Did you ever kiss somebody just because he took you to a great concert?"

"Sure."

"Did you ever fuck him?"

"Sometimes."

"Was it love?"

"No."

"No. He was nice to you, you were nice to him. You fucked him because it made your life better. A nice show, maybe a good meal. Maybe some earrings. Everybody's ready to fuck for something. How about marriage? Those poor girls not only have to fuck the guy, they have to cook and clean too. Forever. And all because he brings in a little money."

"So it's been cool for you?" I ask.

"I'm a different story," Trish says. "I'm stuck here. I'm into that clean morphine and I just can't get up and leave. Pretty soon, though. I'm only gonna do it for a little while longer. I've got some jobs lined up back home, yeah. Right now I'm here and I'm not going any-where. And the dope is ... pharmaceutical."

We are standing outside our hotel room when a tall aristocratic Eng-lish woman strides down the hall followed by a tall pale boyish young man. She stops and claps her hands imperiously. Pakistani men come rushing in, burdened with luggage.

"Come on now," the woman orders, "13, 14, ah, here we are, number 15. With two beds. That's fine. Put all those over here. And we'll have some hot tea. Do you understand? Chi. Hot chi. Yes, thank you. Good bye."

She closes the door. Donna and I look at each other.

"I never saw them jump like that," I say.

"She just clapped her hands," Donna says. "I've seen it before among the uppers."

"I can see why she'd expect them to obey, but why do the hotel guys buy into it?"

A young American comes up the stairs dragging a big suitcase.

"Hey," I say.

"Hey," he says.

"I'm Les. This is Donna."

"Jack."

"Just in, huh?"

"I just landed at the airport. It's long flight from Europe to here."

"How long you gonna be in Pakistan?"

"I'm leaving Wednesday."

Donna says, "Three days from now?"

"Yeah."

"Dope deal!" Donna and I say in unison.

"No. I'm not doing a deal," he says.

"You flew into Pakistan for three days and you're flying home."

"Yeah."

"Dope deal!" we say again in unison.

"No deal," he insists. "I'm just checking the place out for some friends."

"Sure sure," says Donna.

"Maybe I'll see you later," Jack says.

"Sure," says Donna

Jack goes into his room. Suddenly the drunk's radio comes wailing down the hall at the usual volumes. Donna and I go into the room, close the door and begin flicking our light, creating static.

"Well this has worked three nights running. Let's go for a fourth," she says.

But I'm a little worried. "I'm starting to get concerned that eventually even a drunk might notice the correlation between the static and the flickering light from around our door. Let me try something."

I stand on a chair and wrap a t-shirt around the bulb to darken the room. I go to the switch and start to flip the light on and off. The static is screeching but the radio remains on high. I continue to flip the switch. Suddenly the t-shirt bursts into flame. I rush over to grab it, pull it down and beat it out. In the noise and commotion and smoke our door has opened and everyone, including the drunk (the radio has been turned down) are staring in.

"We're fine," I say.

"No problem here," says Donna.

★ ★ ★ ★ ★

That night Angie, the Englishwoman, and Richard, her husband, are sitting with me and Donna in our hotel room.

Angie is speaking in her very upper class way. "Yes Richard and I were just married and we're on our way to the Seychelles."

"Where are the Seychelles?" Donna asks.

"They're islands in the middle of the Indian Ocean. About as far from home as a place can be."

"Is it your honeymoon?" I ask.

"Oh no. We're going there to live for several years."

"And do what?"

"Richard is a poet. He's going to write and I'm going to take care of him."

Donna looks over at the wan young man. "Poet eh? You don't say very much for a poet."

"Richard's quiet. But the words he writes are quite beautiful." Richard smiles slightly.

"A little hash? I offer.

"Pakistani or Afghani?" Angie inquires.

"Pakistani," I say. "I've had enough of the Afghani for a while. I ate quite a bit at the Afghan border."

"Yes," says Angie, "we had a similar experience there."

"You ate hash at the border too?

"Yes," she says. "We had a jeep. I was driving and we had both eaten some hashish we'd bought from a policeman at a chi shop.

"Just like you Lesi," says Donna.

"How did that go?" I ask.

"Well, it was all right for a while but about an hour later Richard was feeling so badly that I had to pull over and he lay down on the ground and we had to stay there for a few hours before he was ready to go on."

"What about you Angie?" Donna says. "Weren't you affected?"

"Well," she says, "I wasn't quite myself."

★ ★ ★ ★ ★

Donna and Jack and I are eating in a Chinese restaurant.

"Thanks for bringing me here," says Jack. "I just can't eat that hot stuff."

"Yeah, we know what you mean. Everything's hot here. Very hot. See this red stuff?" I point to a bowl on the table. "That's straight ground up chillies. Hot ones. The Pakistanis put it in all the dishes when they eat here, just to make it tasty.

"Yeah. Kinda gross. This food is pretty good though."

I say, "Yeah. I thought Chinese restaurants came from New York. Silly I guess. I see now that the Chinese are kind of like the cooks of the planet. No spare ribs here though."

"Not here in Pakistan," says Donna. "So Jack. How about it? Tell us about your deal."

"I told you Donna there's no deal."

"Come on Jack," she pushes him, "you know us by now. We'll keep your secret. What's the deal?"

Jack looks at us for a moment.

"I could use a little help."

"Hah! I knew it," Donna says. "What's the plan Jack?"

"I really need to know I can trust you," he says.

"Come on what's the plan?" Donna's impatient.

"I have some friends back home in Detroit. Very rich friends. Their parents are in the auto industry. They're financing me. They sent me out here to buy a hundred kilos of Pakistani hash."

"A hundred keys?" Donna says.

"Yeah. Its going to be sent to Geneva Switzerland where it's gonna be built into skis."

"You mean like inside the ski?"

"Yeah. Sealed up tight."

"That's brilliant!" cheers Donna.

"And then it gets shipped out to the US and everywhere else."

I'm impressed. "I gotta say, that's pretty good. So what do you need us for?"

"I've made arrangements for the hash, but I just found out it won't be here for a week, and I do not want to stick around that long. Do you know the Metropole Hotel?"

"Yeah. Very posh," says Donna.

"I need you to get a room at the Metropole. Then sometime next week you'll have to go up to another room where the hash will be and check it out. Make sure its good shit and a good weight. And that's it."

I'm thinking this through. "We don't have to carry it anywhere?"

"No, just wire me in Detroit that its cool and I'll send them their money. They'll take care of the rest. And I'll send you a thousand dollars to do it."

"A thousand dollars just to look at it," Donna says.

"You'll have to smoke it too."

"If we stay around another week," I say, "we'll miss our boat to Bombay." It was time for that Greek freighter.

"Fly." says Jack.

"You put all this together in three days?" I ask. "Paid out all the proper baksheesh? Nothing's gonna work unless you pay out all the baksheesh."

"Everybody's paid."

"We'll have to think about this."

"I'd like to leave tomorrow," he says.

The waiter appears with the check.

"That's the other thing," Jack says. "I've spent all my money. All my friend's money too. and I'm about $60 short for my flight. Can you help me with that? And I don't have money for dinner."

★ ★ ★ ★ ★

Later back at the hotel room we are deliberating. "What do you think?" Donna asks

"Well, of course we want to do it. Its just a question of assessing the risk."

"We won't have to carry it anywhere. That's usually the risky part."

"And," I say, "if they find us in the hotel with the hash I think I could talk our way out of that. Its not our room."

"How would we weigh it? A hundred kilos," she says.

"I have a plan for that," I say. "We bring a can of coke and a wooden board with us. We put the hash on one end of the board and place the can of Coke underneath the board as a fulcrum. You weigh, I believe about one hundred and ten pounds?

"That's right." she says.

"That's half of one hundred kilos."

"Is it?"

"Yes 220 pounds. So if we put the can twice as close to the hash as to you, it should all balance out."

"Lesi."

★ ★ ★ ★ ★

We are at the airport. Donna and Jack and I get out of a cab. I pay the driver.

The cab driver says, "I will wait for you."

"OK," I say, "but we might be a while.

"That is no problem," he says. "I will wait."

We walk into the main hall.

"Thanks a lot for bringing me," Jack says.

"So you're going to wire us the thousand on Monday," I say. "If we don't have it by Wednesday we're leaving on the boat Thursday."

"Yes, by Monday," says Jack. "So long Donna."

"Bye bye Jackie. We'll be in touch." She gives him a kiss.

We watch as he reaches immigration and customs who take him into the next room and, of course, ask him to open his luggage. Donna and I go outside to where we can watch him through a large window. Suddenly the cabdriver is at our elbow.

"You better leave. You better leave. Your friend's in trouble," he says, insistent and conspiratorial. "They know he has hashish."

Donna and I smile at each other. "He has no hashish."

"No hashish?" says the cab driver. He looks confused.

"No," I say.

The cabdriver leaves. I turn my attention back to where the officials are opening Jack's luggage. The cabdriver returns.

"You better come quickly. Your friend's in trouble. They know he has the hashish."

Looking back at the cabdriver I am starting to get annoyed. "He has no hash! He has no hash!"

"But he doesssssssssssssss," I hear Donna saying.

I turn and look through the window to where Donna is staring. The customs officials are diving into Jack's luggage. They pull out wadded up dirty laundry. From each piece they pull out a big clear plastic bag of hash.

"Time to go," I say.

We quickly follow the cabdriver back to his cab and get in, but the police are immediately there. They take us from the cab and bring us into a concrete room. They leave us alone.

"That asshole!" Donna is saying. "That stupid boy. What an asshole."

I'm worried. "This could be trouble baby. We can't let them lock you up."

"Yeah. That doesn't sound good. That asshole. What was he thinking? Here for three and a half days and he thinks he can fly out with a suitcase full of hash."

"Dumb," I say. "Let me talk."

An officer comes in. Looks at some papers on his desk.

"Braunstein and Thompson. Is that correct?"

"Yes," I say.

"American and British. But you know that as foreign nationals you are still subject to the laws of my country. And it is illegal to traffic in hashish. The penalties are quite severe. Do you know that? You are facing many years in prison. Both of you." He looks at Donna.

I say, "We know that. That boy out there is a fool. We are not fools. We know better than to try to do such a thing."

"So you are saying you did not know he had hashish?"

"If we knew, would we have waited outside? We would have left immediately or would never have come with him at all."

The officer thinks this over.

"You will have to wait here." He goes out.

"That was good, Les," Donna says. "And its true."

A while later the officer comes back in.

"You are very fortunate. Your friend says the same thing. That you knew nothing about his hashish. We have decided to release you."

"Thank you," I say, very relieved and a little surprised. "May we speak with him before we leave?"

"Yes. Come this way."

He leads us to another room where Jack is sitting at a table.

"Hi guys. Sorry. I'm really sorry."

"You little asshole," says Donna, furious. "You almost got us arrested too."

"I'm really sorry."

"Man you should be," I say. "What a stupid move. So what's gonna happen now? How do you get out of this?"

"They've already started working it out for me," he says. "They tell me I'm gonna need two thousand dollars. That's for my lawyer here and the fine and what he has to pay the judge and the rest of them. I need you to wire my friends in Detroit. They'll send it to you."

"That's fine," I say, "but sticking around doing all this shit for you is going to mean we miss our boat to Bombay, so we'll have to tell them to send our thousand dollars too."

"Yeah, yeah. Sure," says Jack. "They'll do that. That's fine. That's good."

"OK. Write it all down," I say.

"Asshole!" says Donna.

"Sorry."

★★★★★

A week later we are back at Karachi airport. Donna and I are once again seeing Jack off.

"So long, Shit for Brains," says Donna.

"Bye Donna," he says. "You guys have your tickets?"

"Right here. No hash this time, right Jack?"

"No. My lawyer is working that all out for me. This time the right way."

"All the proper baksheesh."

"You bet," says Jack.

His plane is called.

"Bye," he says.

He leaves. Donna and I walk down to the other end of the terminal to where a flight is boarding for Colombo Ceylon.

"Are you ready for this?, she asks me. "Got those tranks from Trish?"

"I took two," I say.

"I still can't believe you got this far around the world without ever taking a plane."

"I always said I would, when the time came."

We board. I sit next to the window. The jets fire and the plane begins to run up the runway. Donna and I look at each other. I'm nervous. Then the plane tilts up and we rush into the sky. I am silent as I watch the clouds pass by. Then we break into the sunshine above the clouds.

"Well?" she asks.

"I love this. This is great."

"Good boy."

Ceylon

Gotta gimme two tickets on the train for Negombo two tickets cause we gotta get back there two tickets on the train on the train —Ticket to Negombo

The airport in Ceylon is about twenty miles north of Colombo, the main city. But Donna and I had had enough of cities for a while, so we turned north, and went up to the nearby fishing village of Negumbo.

Ceylon. You can't go there anymore. It's like Constantinople in that sense. Like the song says – Can't go back to Constantinople, now it's Istanbul, not Constantinople. At some point in the intervening years, Ceylon became Sri Lanka. Hey, that's their choice. Ceylon might just have been a Brit mispronunciation . But I am happy to have been one of the last visitors to the magical Island of Ceylon.

A rickety taxi took us up the coast. The sea to our left was dotted with boats. Hollowed out logs with sails. The prettiest boats I had ever seen. Each boat had two masts and a big square sail. They appeared in clusters on the ocean horizon. To our right tall palm trees rose up at the edge of the jungle. The taxi was taking us to someone who could arrange for a place to stay in Negumbo. Did we want to go to the very big hotel, he inquired No? OK. He had a friend. The friend had a little storefront in the village. We sat down in a room with only a desk and some chairs. A boy ran out to get tea. Lovely young girls draped in silks peered in at us from the doorways and giggled. They were so beautiful to see. Like cherubs after the lands we had been in. Laughing cherubs with long legs and sun-brown skin. They wore a simple wrap that barely covered them from breast to thigh. What a relief. Women need to hold more power in the world. That influence will be a great change for humankind. But women's presence alone warmed me and made me feel good. It had nothing to do with sex. I was not going to fuck these women. I was traveling with a dream girl. But just having these girls near and visible. Their laughs, their legs. Well maybe sex had something to do with it. Anyway, I felt good just seeing them there.

The man once again suggested that we stay at the big hotel. There was only one at that time. Some big European corporation had built it on the beach just up from the village. It was new and it had lots of empty rooms and we could stay there for a very reasonable rate.

No thank you we said. We wanted to stay for at least a month, and even a reasonable hotel rate of 15 or 20 dollars a day would add up to too much. And we wanted something away from everyone else. But also on the beach. Was there some thing like that? A little hut or something we could rent? Ahh, said the man. Let me see what I can do. Please go and walk around the village and return in one hour.

When we returned an hour later he told us that a judge who lived in Colombo had a little cottage on the beach and was not currently using it. It was about half a mile up the coast, situated on the shore of a coconut plantation. No electricity and a hand pump for water. We could rent that for $60 for the month. Would we like to see it? Yes we would.

Donna taking pictures

So we moved into a little house on the beach. There was nobody around but tall coconut palm trees, sand, and the ocean singing outside our windows. Did I mention that it faced west and the sun set over the ocean for us each day as we sat on our porch?

We each wore only a towel, a wrap. That's all anyone wore in Ceylon. For hours we hung in the warm sea, talking, touching. We ate dinner watching the sun as it set. When darkness came we climbed together into our bed. I kissed her and licked the salt off her lips, her breasts, her cunt. She reciprocated fully. We were as close as humans can be.

★ ★ ★ ★ ★

We didn't venture very far. A little stroll would take you into the village. Vendors with carts sold coconuts that they would hack open with a machete for you to drink. Coconut milk isn't that creamy stuff you put into piña coladas. It's a refreshing sweet water. Delicious and pure. Pure because it's sealed up until opened in front of you, they sometimes had the Western innovation of a plastic straw. But usually you just tilted it back and enjoyed.

Our world now is chock full of things to eat and drink. You have your favorites and they are almost always available. So there's not much chance someone will be opening a coconut for you soon. And the whole machete thing would seem a little dangerous. But where there is none of that stuff, no cokes or beers, just water that you'd better boil, being handed a coconut by a smiling toothless man, and feeling that pure sweet juice run over your tongue down your throat..... well that just tastes better than any specialty drink from a skilled barister.

Mangoes. I had eaten a mango or two before. Pretty good. Now look at these little things. They were yellow and small, like an elongated lemon. But they were soft and so sweet. Peach-like with a hint of lemon and banana when you scrape the skin with your teeth. The best fruit I had ever eaten. Ten of these little guys cost a dime.

Sometimes we would go to the market and buy fish, fresh from the sea. One day we saw what looked like a large hunk of roast beef or pork. Red and completely lean. The back end of it was a fish's tail.

"What's this?" I asked the fish man.

"That is Sea Pig. Sea Pig." said his friend who spoke a little English. It did in fact look like pork. But there was this black fishtail.

"Shark? Swordfish? It's not a porpoise is it?"

"Sea Pig. You want some?"

I looked at Donna who nodded. "Yeah. Give us some Sea Pig please."

The man spoke to the fish man who held his knife to show me what he would be cutting. I held up two fingers and the man quickly cut two big steaks of red meat.

Back at the cottage I start our fire on the beach and go over to a table outside to prepare the steaks. I have salt and some spices I have found in the market. I rub them in. I've bought some peppers at the market, too. The woman has told me they are sweet, when I had asked. I haven't wanted any hot spicy dishes since leaving Pakistan. I chop the peppers finely and put them and some onions into a large black frying pan that has come with the house. I stop for a moment and go across the yard and pee into the trees. I am walking back to the table when something starts to happen. My cock! Is .. burning! What the fuck? The fucking peppers. They're hot after all. I've handled them and then held my cock and now.... The burning is growing more and more intense. I look around frantically.

"Lesi. What's wrong?"

"Ahhh. Yaaaa."

"What?"

"Hot peppers! On my cock!"

For a second she looks bewildered and then she begins to laugh.

"Its not funny!" I look around again, rip off my towel and run into the ocean. I desperately wash my hands in the seawater before I dare to touch my prick. My balls are burning now too.

Even in the ocean it takes a couple of minutes for the burning to subside completely. I walk out of the water to where Donna is waiting on the shore. She tries but is unable to stop laughing.

"It's not funny."

"I know. Sorry." She tries to look concerned for a second, then just gives up and laughs. I want to be pissed but then I am laughing too.

And the sea pig. Delicious.

I was out floating in the night sea. There was a high intensity phosphorescence in the water. If you dragged your hands quickly through the water a bright trail of phosphors glowed in its wake. Kicking your feet churned up bursts of light. I had been thinking about my mother. She had never been anywhere but New York, Atlantic City or Miami Beach. I was spending my money on friends. Why not spend a little on Mom. Blow her mind a little. So I sent her a letter and told her that if she wanted to, I'd buy her a round trip ticket to Tel Aviv and I'd meet her in Israel on my way back to London. That would get her some extra respect around the condo's pool in Miami. And anyway, it was all kind of a grandstand play. What were the chances she'd say yes?

There were elephants around. Not just for show. These were worker elephants. They would come through occasionally, two or three of them being ridden by their handlers. They would go over to where a palm tree had fallen over, pick it up in their trunks and drag it over to a pile. Sometimes two elephants would work together with a very large tree. But a single elephant is capable of dragging off a pretty massive palm tree. They were exactly like heavy equipment back home. Like bulldozers and front loaders. The handlers kept up a steady stream of clackings and shouts. Occasionally one would clonk on his elephant's head with a heavy stick to get it's attention, but there was clearly a close relationship between the men and the big beasts. When they stopped for a rest the elephants would nuzzle their men, imploring them for snacks. When they stood in the creek nearby they sprayed each other and the men. Playing.

The Ceylonese people were very nice. It was around then that I began to truly understand the difference that you felt as you moved from culture to culture. Each culture, each religion really, had a different state of mind, which affected the congeniality of the people. Here in my travels I had suddenly gone from a Muslim country to a Hindu country and the difference was everywhere. I was to discover that in Hindu and Buddhist countries the people were, in a general and a personal way, more sweet and cooperative. Wherever we went, people smiled and tried to be helpful.

I came across a place in the village that sold kites. Ceylonese kites are two piece things that look like bats or birds. I remembered how hard I often had to work to get a kite up in the air when I was a kid. These Ceylonese kites...You held them up and they shot straight up into the sky. No muss. No fuss. Just bang up into the sky. I'm gonna say it. Their kites are better than ours. Maybe they have kites like these everywhere now. I hope so.

One afternoon Donna and I went into a batik shop. Donna wanted something local and nice to wrap around her. The colors were beautiful. The Ceylonese were world famous for their fabrics. I sat down at a little table while Donna shopped. Some young women gave me tea and giggled. I picked up an Indian magazine and a photo fell out. It was a photo of John Paul George and Ringo. I was very surprised. Where had this come from? I asked the women, "Do you know who this is?" They looked, and one responded, "They are your brothers?" "Yes", I said, and with their permission I took the picture and have it to this day.

My brothers – from the collection of the girls in batik shop in Negombo

After almost a month had gone by, we decided it was time to check out Colombo. Negombo had clearly been the right place to start, but still, Colombo was only an hour away. We didn't like to pass anything up. Maybe Colombo would be even better than Negombo. It didn't sound likely but... So we got two tickets on the train and went to town.

We came out of the station in Colombo and began walking down a broad white street that led to the waterfront. There would be some big hotel there where we could have a nice lunch. There were a lot of cars. Really a lot. In Negombo it had been rickshaws and oxcarts. As we started down the boulevard we quickly realized that we had no shoes on. We hadn't worn shoes in several weeks. There was nowhere you could go in Negombo where that mattered, but here, suddenly it did. Our feet were frying on the hot white pavement. We had forgotten that we might need city feet. We limped towards a big hotel, basically dashing from grassy spot to grassy spot. We made it, hurting, to the hotel's front door.

"No! I am very sorry," says the doorman, "but it is not possible being in here with no shoes."

"Please," says Donna. "It's so hot and my feet hurt so much. See.. Ow ow ow." She hops around for him demonstrating pain.

"Sorry. I can not let you in here with your no shoes."

"Thanks," I say.

We walk around the back and notice that there is a snack bar by the pool. No one will care about shoes here. We sit down and a waiter comes over.

"Yes. What can I bring you please?" he says.

Donna is getting excited by the menu. "I'll have a grilled cheese sandwich."

"Oh man, me too," I say. "First grilled cheese in a long long time."

"And I'll have the English tea with jam," says Donna.

"One of those for me, too."

The waiter says, "Two grilled sandwiches with cheese, two English teas with the jam. Your room please?"

"No room. We'll pay for it here."

"No room? What number please?"

"No," I say, "we have no room here. We will pay you this money now." I dig into a sack at my waist and show the waiter that we have money.

"No. I am very sorry but I can not be serving you unless you are having a room here in this hotel. Or if you would like you can be making arrangements for a one day pool pass inside at the lobby."

"We can't go into the lobby because we have no shoes."

"Yes. But perhaps you are buying some shoes at a nice shop up this road."

"Grilled cheese," moans Donna.

I look at Donna who looks at me.

"Negombo?" I say.

"There's a train in twenty minutes," she says.

"All aboard."

Monday, March 22

Dear son — what a day. I don't think I shall ever forget it. Tears of joy. A letter from my Les. October 31 was the last time I heard from you. After I dashed off a letter immediately to Peshawar I came back to my apartment and sat there in the dark. It was Holloween and I remembered past happy Halloweens in which you played a very vital part, especially when you were a wee young one and wore my kelly green jacket and that shiny green high hat and were the mad Hatter, and so many many occasions that gave us such pleasure. One week later we heard about the tidal wave that wrought such destruction in Pakistan. Not knowing the country we all were terribly concerned about you. A good friend brought me several books and maps on Asia and he convinced me that Dacca was a great distance from Peshawar. I realized that you couldn't possibly have gotten that far on a horse. We didn't know how vast Pakistan really is. But then after several weeks of no word from you that old worry started up again. About a month ago I called the Special Service for Civilians Abroad in Washington and spoke to the head of the department. The woman in charge told me that they couldn't possibly trace you since I knew not where you were headed. And she said records are so loosely kept in Pakistan they would not be able to find you unless you were in some trouble and the American Consul would then be notified and I in turn would be informed so "no news is good news." I lived with the hope that someday soon I would receive a letter from you. Today is that blessed day. I read the letter to Ann and Morris Silverstein and they too shed tears of joy with me. I've been walking around with that silly grin and tears running down my cheeks. I am indeed a happy mother.

I want you to know — A team of horses can't keep me from you. I am coming to Israel.

The next day a man came up the beach with lobsters. He was going up to the big hotel to sell them, but he was happy to sell a couple to us for 25 cents each. Of course, there was going to be the usual problem with lobsters – the killing thing. I decided to take the coward's way out and just left them to die in a basket on the porch. We spent the afternoon in the village. When we came home we discovered that the lobsters had tried to make a break for it and had crawled halfway across the beach toward the surf. To my eternal shame, I picked them up and put them back on the porch. I should have thrown them into the sea. By evening they were dead. I dug a pit in the sand and built a fire. Then I took the two lobsters and threw them in. They immediately began writhing in pain and I had the opportunity to face the death that I took for granted whenever I ate meat. Good for me. And actually the lobsters turned out pretty good too. A lesson learned, a dinner enjoyed.

Sunset from our hut on the beach in Negombo

Day after day
drops away
like the sun that burns a red goodbye
and drops beyond the sea – journal

A few afternoons later I was bobbing in the sea. The sunset was just beginning. The sun was still well above the horizon, but the sky above was already filled with pinks and oranges reaching out in rays from the mother star. I looked toward the West and I thought about home. I was now on the other side of my planet. It had taken close to two years to get halfway around, and it was likely to take me another two if I kept going at this pace. Two more years till I had a chance to be home, in America. The chance to play my songs. I wanted that. I had written a lot during my travels. I felt like I finally knew a few things, had something worth telling, worth putting into a song. I had seen more of the world than most people and I was... optimistic. I felt that things could work out for my stupid species and I wanted to say that.

Now that people like Donna and I could travel like this, cross the world, come face to face with the world, we could pass the secret along. That we're all people. All the same. Foreigners are not beasts who do not matter. They are people with families like yours much the same as you.

And in carrying this vision, travelers knit the world together. Never before in the history of the planet had so many people traveled so extensively. Travelers see the world, and the world sees them.

And in that moment I decided to turn around and head toward home.

We took a walk down the shore to see the big hotel. We hadn't been there yet. It turned out to be a giant thing, right on the beach, almost no one around. As we approached we saw there was a portly older European man in a bathing suit sitting on the patio.

Donna says, "Walter?"

Donna and Walter in front of the big hotel in Negombo

The man stands up and looks at her.

"Donna?" he says.

They run to each other and hug like the best old friends.

"Lesi, Lesi, this is Walter. He used to be the manager at the hotel in Scotland where my sister was working and where I grew up. Walter, what are you doing here?"

(In a heavy Austrian accent) "I am the manager here. The hotel was just built by a Swiss company and they send me here to open it for them."

"I'm so glad to see you. I can't believe it. Walter is like my favorite uncle."

"Yah, it's true."

"And my sister's very very favorite." He reddens.

"And what do you do here?" Walter asks.

"Les and I are just traveling. Seeing a bit of the world."

"Hi Walter," I say.

"Well come stay with me," he says. "Sit down. What do you drink?"

"I'll take a gin and tonic," say Donna. "First drink in a while."

"Do you have a Courvoisier?" I ask.

"I'm sure we do." He calls over a waiter and orders. "So really, where are you staying?"

"We're just up the beach at a little cottage," she says.

"Well now you must come here. I will make it very cheap and you know it's too dangerous now to stay out there."

"Dangerous? Why?"

"Because of the rebellion. You have not heard? The Tamil Tigers, Muslim separatists are fighting with the government. It is a real war now. You must stay here. Look, all my guests have been evacuated. You should have been also. Now the airport is closed."

"Nobody told us."

"You're the only travelers left. You must move in here."

"You know Walter," says Donna, " I think we'll be OK. There's nothing like that going on in Negombo."

"Well if you change your mind, you have a room here. And now you will eat the most expensive meal in Negombo for no charge."

"I'll drink to that," I say.

And we do.

★ ★ ★ ★ ★

It was dark when we got home. We were getting ready for bed when...

"Les. Did you hear that?"

"Yeah. There's someone outside."

We wait. There's a tentative knock on the door. I open it to see two young men on the porch and two others just beyond in the dark. Do they have rifles?"

"Yes?" I say.

"Hello. We did not think there was anyone here," says the first young man.

"We are living here."

"We were hoping to spend the night here," he says.

He is soft spoken and intelligent. He looks over toward Donna. "But..."

"Yes," I say, "you can see that you can not stay here. I'm sorry."

I close the door and we look at each other. There is a sudden banging at the door. I pull it open. A second man comes forward and speaks angrily.

"We will stay here! There is a curfew. Anyone on the roads will be shot. We are not from here and have no place else to go."

I think about having four armed men spending the night here with me and Donna. Can't happen. I suss immediately that this second guy is not going to listen to me so I turn back to the first. (A little trick I learned from JFK during the missile crisis.)

"You can not stay here. My first job is to protect this woman and you can not stay here. You know it would not be proper or right."

The first begins to speak with the second.

"No!" says the second. "We will stay here!"

Again I speak directly to the first. "We have heard there is a rebellion. I don't know your fight. You may be right or you may be wrong. I do not know. But you know you should not bring us into this. This is your land. Find a place with your people."

At this the first man looks at me for a long few seconds, then he turns and walks out. The second objects strongly but they all follow the first off the porch and into the night.

Donna and I latch the door and close the shutters on all the windows. Then I tie pots and pans to every window and door so we will hear if anyone tries to open them.

We sit fully clothed on our bed and listen. For a while we can still hear the men outside. Then quiet. The next morning we move into the hotel.

It turned out that we were not the only people staying at the hotel. There were Russian "technicians" who had just turned up to help out the Ceylonese government with something or other and there were Americans from the "World Bank". The Americans were obviously CIA and the Russians probably KGB. They had all been sent there at a moment's notice to keep their eyes on the situation and each other and that turned out to mean drinking and playing ping pong. Both groups were very interested in (suspicious of) me and Donna. As Walter had said, all the other travelers and tourists had been evacuated. There wasn't much to spy on except the two of us and each other. And the Chinese warships. The Chinese had rushed a sizable armada out to hang off the coast and keep an eye on things from there. The horizon was full of them. I didn't know much about warships, but this was definitely a significant fleet.

I was having a recurrence of my mouth sores, and lacking any ginseng was bathing my mouth with Walter's Courvoisier. The Russian guys were young and fascinated by Donna. Russian women were far more independent than some around the globe. But these guys had never seen anything like this one. Especially when they learned that she had started her travels on her own, not under the protection of me or any other man. They themselves had no such opportunity for independence. She could also drink like a man (better than I who was usually Courvoisiated by mid evening) and was extremely attractive so they were all half in love with her within a few days. The Americans were older and acted in a more paternalistic way. It took them a few days to be convinced that we had no purpose other than pure travel and the love of life, which these guys seemed to consider a waste of time. After a few days the "World Bank" guys ignored us and mostly sat and drank. I played ping pong with the young Russians and argued politics. The thrust of the Russian position was that much of the world was backwards and needed the Soviets to bring them modernity, whereupon these countries should forever revere Mother Russia as their savior and leader. It wasn't a new idea to me, I'd certainly heard that often enough from my own leader/buffoons. The Russians castigated me for America's folly in Viet Nam. I didn't hesitate to agree. Unfortunately in a few years some of these same young Russians would be dead in Afghanistan. (Followed by more young Americans.)

For another week we floated in the warm sea and dreamed and watched clusters of square-sailed dugout boats.

Then Walter told us that the airport had reopened and flights were available to India. Donna and I figured we had experienced the best Ceylon had had to offer. It had been as close to paradise as anything either of us had ever known. But exotic India was calling to us. We tried to pay our hotel and bar bill but it had somehow become lost. Donna hugged Walter goodbye and we said goodbye to our fellow guests. The Americans were uninterested but polite. The Russians seemed a little heartbroken that we were leaving. Donna, of course, but even I had affected them. We seemed so impossibly free.

At the airport we found there was a flight leaving for Madras. We took it. The first step toward home.

Acknowledgments

Every writer needs a great place to sit and write. I'd like to thank Carolyn Sue and Valentino, my wife and my Westie for my spot between our Ulster County farmhouse and our pond where I sat and did nothing but this.

And also the fabulous ArtBoy, Geno, who opened his homes and studios to me in a garden courtyard in San Miguel D'Allende, in a glass room overlooking the ocean on Islabella, an island off the coast of Brazil, and in his loft in Soho where we laughed and talked and I wrote most of the rest.

And to my kids Michael and Allison who keep me moving forward like some addlebrained shark. Allison helping with graphics and tech and Michael lending me his rock band to sing in front of.

Printed in Great Britain
by Amazon

77575765R00098